Good News
for Bad Days

Good News
for Bad Days

Living a Soulful Life

FATHER PAUL KEENAN

WARNER BOOKS

A Time Warner Company

Warner Books, Inc., 1271 Avenue of the Americas, New York, NY 10020
Visit our Web site at http://warnerbooks.com

 A Time Warner Company

First Printing: May 1998
10   9   8   7   6   5   4   3   2   1

Library of Congress Cataloging-in-Publication Data

Keenan, Paul.
    Good news for bad days : living a soulful life / Paul Keenan.
        p.   cm.
    ISBN 0–446–52156–6
    I. Christian life—Catholic authors.   2. Keenan, Paul.   I. Title.
BX2350.2.K425   1998
248.4'82—dc21   97–18434
                                                           CIP

Contents

Chapter One

You Can Get There from Here

I have all this success. What I don't have is a life!" The young executive sitting across the dinner table from me was the picture of prosperity. Youthful, handsome, in radiant health, he appeared to be enjoying the good life. No one among his closest friends or business associates would have dreamed of his uttering those words. To be sure, he was the envy of many of them. Yet there he was, candidly admitting that something very important was missing. What was missing, he was telling me, was his life.

As I listened to him, I knew what he meant. I have at times watched my own life spin away from me in a flurry of appointments, deadlines, trains to catch, programs to prepare, things to do. There have been times when, like my dinner companion that evening, I too have wondered, "Where is my life?"

When that question rears its ugly head, I often feel like I am caught in one of those nightmares where I try and try to get out of a burning room or to run away from a monster, but I cannot find the knob to open the door. The harder I try, the closer to danger I feel. I want desperately to get to safety, but the message of the dream haunts me: "You can't get there from here."

How do we get to the place called soul when we feel trapped in our lives?

One of the most important discoveries of my adult life has been the discovery of my having options. I was in my thirties, I guess, before I began to become aware of that ongoing feeling of defeat that comes from a sense of being trapped. For a long time, I couldn't put it into words—it was just there. As time went on, I became angrier, more irritable, for no apparent reason. When I was finally able to find the words to express what I was feeling, I realized that I had spent my life doing what other people wanted me to do and not doing what I wanted. What did I want? I didn't know. I honestly didn't know. All I could tell you was that I wasn't happy.

Looking back on this experience from the vantage point of fifteen years, it is easy to see where it was leading. Now I know that I was being led out of dreams of academia, out of my life in the Jesuits, into the life of a parish priest in the Archdiocese of New York, into communications and radio and public speaking and writing, into a life of real freedom. But back then, I didn't have a clue about any of that.

In fact, had I, in my unfocused anger and dissatisfaction, up and changed my life to the one I have now, I still would not have found my soul. The real change had to be made within. And as I can see fifteen years later, it had to be made in a very special way, not by arbitrarily changing everything all at once.

At the time, however, I had no such clarity of vision. I felt that I was groping around in a pea-soup fog. I felt like a failure, and I felt that others thought of me as a failure. Would I ever be able to get out? Would I ever amount to anything?

The key that opened the door to my soul for me was the realization that I could make choices and that I had options. Now, that sounds like the silliest thing in the world. Of course I had been making decisions all my life. No one had walked beside me through life holding a shotgun to my head. But telling myself that my feelings were silly did not make them go away. I had to take time and find out what they had to say.

As I listened to my feelings, I realized that over the years, I had developed a lack of confidence in my ability to make choices, and that more often than not I had learned to make decisions based on the strong beliefs of others as to what was right for me. Deep down, I had come to the point where I felt that I could not change my life, that I was stuck with it, that I had to suppress my own wishes. I did not know clearly what my own wishes were.

The most important learning for me was that in almost every situation in my life, I had a range of options I could consider. When I was asked to do particular things, there was a variety of ways for me to respond. I learned that in order not to feel trapped, I had to stop and ask myself, "What are my options here?" and look for two or three different ways to respond. Down the road, this helped me a great deal in making the important decision to leave the Jesuits and to become a priest of the Archdiocese of New York. Before, I might have sulked angrily and held on, or at some point thrown everything over in utter frustration. Now I could slow down, take my time, look at various ways of dealing with my situation, and decide calmly and serenely what to do.

The upshot was that I made better decisions. In

the long run, something even more wonderful happened. Instead of being resentful and angry, I discovered a growing peace of soul.

When we are stuck in life, feeling angry and resentful and trapped, we can ask ourselves, "What are my options here?" Doing that, we can make our world open up, with new horizons. Plus, we get in touch with the movement of our soul deep within us.

It is sad that more of us do not realize that the soul has a voice that calls and guides us throughout our lives. The good news is that more people are turning within for soulful guidance. The soul is the Godlike aspect of ourselves whereby we can say that we are made in God's image and likeness. When we feel trapped, stuck in our lives, the feeling is a cry for help. It is the cry of a soul that is being muffled. When we feel abandoned by others, abandoned by God, often it is our soul crying to be unshackled.

What are some of the symptoms of that cry?

One symptom is *fatigue*. We find ourselves tired, exhausted. Our energy is being taken in the wrong direction, or is trapped in a vicious circle. After a while, we become spent. Our energy is blocked. Often we find it difficult to sleep and to replenish our energy, and we find ourselves turning to artificial means of stimulation in an effort to replace the energy that has been spent.

Anger can be another sign of being stuck. When we are caught in a pattern of activity, of habit, of need, we may find ourselves increasingly frustrated over our situation. We may feel we are working very hard and getting nowhere. We may feel that the goals we strive for are eluding us while other people are achieving theirs easily. We may begin to blame others for our apparent lack of success and may find ourselves becoming easily impatient or hurt by the words or deeds of others. We may feel that life is unfair, that we are getting bad breaks, that people are out to get us. We are angry, and if our anger is deep-seated enough, it can become blind rage.

Another sign of being stuck is *restlessness*. We speak of feeling "at sixes and sevens" or "at sea." We are adrift in life and do not know where to turn. Desperate for a safe port or haven, we may find ourselves making foolish mistakes, turning to substances that or people who in the long run do not prove helpful to us. We experience a lack of direction, almost as if we do not know where we come from or where we are going.

When we are stuck, we often find ourselves being *fearful*. We are afraid of losing what we have. We are afraid we won't get what we want. We are afraid of what others will think of us. We are afraid of success. We are afraid of failure. In time, we become afraid of our own shadow. Fear keeps us stuck in our ruts. We are afraid to get out, and we are afraid that we will not be able to get out.

Stuck in our ruts, we may find ourselves becoming *bored*. Being stuck, our horizons are limited; and after a while we begin to feel we have nowhere to go. There is no escape, no exit, no matter where we look. Worse, there seems to be no point in our pursuing anything else. Boredom of this kind can lead to *depression*.

If those are the feelings that are associated with being stuck, what might be some of our reactions to those feelings? A prime reaction is *denial*. Just as there is inertia in physical objects, so there is inertia in souls. We do not want to know that we are on a dead-end street. Having worked long and hard to get where we are, we are certainly not inclined to be told that all our efforts have landed us in a cul-de-sac. "It's just a passing phase," we tell ourselves. "It's only a slump. Everybody has them. Things will pick up in a day or two." We will do almost anything to avoid having to change our present patterns in any kind of deep way.

Sooner or later, denial gives way to a vague murky feeling, an obscure malaise. Something is not quite right, and we are beginning to feel it. Strange, we are doing the same things we have always been doing; but now there is no satisfaction, or certainly less satisfaction. We find ourselves sort of mucking around in life, kind of restless, at odds and ends. At this point, we have to come to a decision about what is going on with us. Either we are going to live with the restlessness and the present situation, or we are going to do something about it. Living with it will eventually lead to a kind of cynicism or even depression, the feeling that we are on the short end of life's beneficence. The bounty of life, the realization of the heart's desires, is something that happens only to other people, not to ourselves. Believing this, we can become jaded, feeling that somehow life is out to get us. For a long time, this can be a vague belief that we just live with. Eventually, it may become a firm belief, one that we acknowledge and defend. "One of these days, we'll win the lotto," we tell ourselves. But we really don't believe it.

When it gets to this point, we have a decision to make. Either we are going to accept our malaise as an ongoing condition or we are going to perceive it as an invitation to change. And indeed, there is the rub. When we find ourselves getting stuck, we eventually have to make a decision about where that is going to take us. Will we stay stuck, or will we look for options?

When we choose to listen to the messages that we are receiving from our soul and pay attention to the ways in which we have been reacting to those messages, we awaken to our possibilities. Instead of mucking around, doing the same old thing and growing ever more hopelessly tired of it, we un-shackle the soul and allow it to be free.

When this happens, an interesting change takes place. Whereas before we ignored our symptoms or viewed them as obstacles to our getting any-where, now we treat them as important messages to be listened to, as potential bearers of clues for our journey in life.

There is a story in the Book of Genesis about a stranger who commences to wrestle with Jacob. Jacob appears to be winning, so the stranger pro-ceeds to dislocate Jacob's hip. Since he is still los-ing, the stranger begs Jacob to let him go. Jacob replies, "I will not let you go unless you bless me." Jacob then learns that he has been wrestling with God.

There are two remarkable things about Jacob's story. One is the tremendous strength with which he defends himself, a strength that does not go away when Jacob suffers. How often our suffering brings out a strength in us we did not know we had. The other is that in the midst of his wrestling and his suffering, Jacob refuses to end the match unless he receives a blessing from the one who is wrestling him.

When life wrestles with us, what if at the same time we were to wrestle with all our might and ask a blessing from the one we are struggling with? Viktor Frankl, suffering the horror of the concentration camps, finds strength in Nietzsche's words "Anyone with a why to live for can put up with almost any how," and finds a meaning for himself even in the depths of darkness. St. Lawrence, in the midst of being martyred on an excruciating grill, tells his torturers, "Why don't you turn me over now? I think I'm done on this side," and finds humor as well as sanctity in the flames.

Whether it be in the loving commitment of a parent raising small children, in the constant bedside presence of a wife to a dying husband, in the struggle of a professional man or woman to remain honest at work as he or she struggles to make a living and support his or her family—wherever suffering rears its head and demands sacrifice, there Jacob wrestles, and there Jacob asks a blessing before the battle can end.

Stuck in suffering—as we will find ourselves at least once in our lifetimes and perhaps for an unbearable length of time—we become unstuck only when we face the suffering for the messenger that it is, engage it, and ask it to bless us.

Looked at from the viewpoint of soul, being stuck in suffering has a special importance, a special place in human life. It teaches us that, viewed rightly, our symptoms and our soul can work together.

Rather than being occasions of panic and discouragement, our points of being stuck are what we bring to the table of life. They are the data of our lives, no more, no less. The experience of being stuck gives us the opportunity to pause, to reflect, and to map the journey we have been undertaking, and to seek our options. And that is a very important thing for us to do. When we experience ourselves being stuck, instead of digging ourselves ever deeper into the trench, we can take time to examine where we have been and to ask ourselves whether there are new options for us. Have we accumulated more and more dead weight in our souls? Are there some things, some persons, some places we need to release? Are there patterns of behavior that we need to change? What possibilities for new life lie ahead?

The feeling of being stuck need not be a destructive one. In and of itself, it is no more than a record of what has happened in our lives, and a cry for the future. We can take the opportunity to ask ourselves what limits we want to surpass, what new directions we want to pursue. It can be a call to adventure, to new horizons and new life. You *can* get there from here.

Chapter Two

Your Soul Is Where You Are

*F*inding your soul means getting to the heart of the processes of living and knowing. It means getting beyond the superficial things that happen, even beyond the "wisdom" that "everybody knows" about what life is supposed to be like. It means getting down to the deepest groundings of life. How can we gain access to this dimension of our experience?

When we catch on to the fact that there is a deeper dimension to our lives, a place called soul, we often worry ourselves excessively about trying to define the soul, trying to find it, capture it, determine its location. Especially in this information age, we love to define things and to have everything in its place; and we long to define the soul as well.

Now, we can certainly find philosophical definitions of the soul. We can say that it is the principle of life or call it the seat of our knowledge and love. It is good to have such definitions to aid our understanding. Yet if we are talking about finding our soul in the midst of the vagaries of life, and about living soulfully, those definitions do not bring us into the heart of soulfulness. Like so much of life, souls can be defined but do not succumb fully to definition. They have an elusive quality about them, at once intriguing and maddening.

I love the image that Victor Hugo uses to describe our souls. "Nothing," he says, "is so like a soul as a bee. It goes from flower to flower as a soul from star to star, and it gathers honey as a soul gathers light." The soul is the part of ourselves that gathers light. In that sense, it is like the eyes. But the soul does not duplicate the work of the eyes, gathering sunlight and lamplight within itself. No, the light that the soul gathers is an inner light.

"The eyes are the windows of the soul," we say. We know the difference between those whose eyes are alive and bright and those whose eyes are dull and listless and weary. The sunlight and lamplight those eyes gather are the same in both persons. The difference is in something inner, something interior. The eyes of soulful people have an inner glow. It is even true of animals. One autumn night, I held in my arms a dying cat, a cat I had known for ten years and who had become a special friend. As I held Kitty Taylor and stroked her and spoke soothingly to her, her gaze met mine and held me in an expression of pure love. I had seen that look before, in the eyes of favorite hospital patients whom I visited, and in my mother's eyes just before she died. I have seen it in the eyes of mothers as they speak of the accomplishments of their children, in the eyes of my friend Alberto who takes such enormous pride in his work of choosing and selecting frames for works of art. That soulful look is the same: Although their worlds are so vastly different, each of them has found an inner light. In lovers, I have heard those eyes called "soft eyes." They are the eyes of soul.

I think of Gabrielle, a dear friend from my early days on New York's Lower East Side. Gabrielle, a brilliant German physician, somehow—I never quite understood the exact circumstances—became a street person and finally a resident of the Catholic Worker. She came to our church, and one day something I said, God knows what or how, struck a chord in her heart. She approached me, and I looked into her eyes—nearly blind, she could not see mine—and something deep within us made us friends forever.

I remember long evenings sitting in a parlor or around the kitchen table or in a corner at the Worker, listening with fascination as Gabrielle spoke in a thick German accent of the concentration camps and the husband and adored little boy whom she lost there; of what it was like to hold a bar of soap in her hand and to realize that it was made of the tortured bodies of her people. Though cancer slowly began to claim her ever-skeletal body, her crackly voice would ring with laughter at a joke. The Fourth of July was no joke. Gabrielle would crawl beneath the bed and cringe and scream with terror as the fireworks exploded like the bombs she remembered.

And then there were Mahler and Bach and Mozart. I never knew how she managed it, but from time to time, Gabrielle would appear with cassette recordings, gifts of music so that I would hear and enjoy the music she loved to remember. They were new—just bought—and always the finest recording of each work available. Imagine.

Gabrielle was pure soul. For seventy-four years, an invisible bee within her drew light from the darkness and more than darkness that encompassed the extinction of her people. "I am a witness, and now you are a witness," she told me. "You must never forget."

Clearly, Gabrielle's soulfulness lay in her ability to remember. But that would have meant nothing had her soul not been at work throughout her life, gathering pollen from every moment, every beauty, every unspeakable tragedy, just as it was unfolding before her. Attention is the hallmark of the soul.

The magic of soul is that it can gather light even in moments of unmentionable pain. When we, in our highly technological society, try to fix our pain and fix our lives and do everything in our power to avoid the depths of life, we figuratively swat the bee that can make the only honey that really matters.

One Saturday night, a young woman (let's call her Maria) phoned my radio show and told me she was deeply depressed. She was a former nurse, forty-five years of age, and had spent the last nine years caring for her elderly mother, who had recently died. Now she was totally unable to get out of bed, due to the profound depression she felt over her mother's death. She could not motivate herself to do her taxes, to go through her mother's things, to meet with her cousin who had expressed an interest in helping her, to do the weekly shopping. I tried to suggest to her that perhaps she could come to see me in my office, thinking that if I could get her to do that, at least a partial victory over her bedridden condition might be won. Nothing doing. The distance from Long Island to my Manhattan office was "too far" for her and involved using the Long Island Railroad, which she would not even think of doing.

At that moment, it dawned on me that I was doing what everyone else was doing to her: telling her that she should not be where she was. What if, instead, I encouraged her to stay right where she was, and to honor that?

"How much money do you have?" I asked her.

She was startled by the question.

"How much money do you have? Do you have enough to live on, without working?"

"Well, yes," she replied. "I can't not work forever, but I have enough money for the time being."

"Well," I told her, "it seems to me you are where you want to be. You are in a position to do exactly what you want. You don't want to work, and you are in a financial position to stay home all day and lie in bed. Many people would love to be able to do that and can't. You have the luxury of living the life you want: You can stay home and mourn your mother. This is an excellent time for you to honor your very understandable desire to grieve. Why not simply take advantage of it?"

"But I can't just stay home all day," she retorted. "I ought to be up and doing."

"Well," I said, "that's entirely up to you. Perhaps the day will come when you'll be ready to get out of bed and get dressed and get a job and tend to things. But right now, you're very lucky: You are living exactly the life you want right now. How many people can say that?"

"But I really should get out of bed."

As so often happens, we ended the conversation without coming to a firm resolution of what she would do. But I found it extremely interesting that once she was given permission to be where she was, she began to see for herself that she might want something more for her life. In fact, Maria calls me from time to time and is now beginning to take the steps that will enable her to move forward with her life.

The approach that I used with her shocks many people today, in this age of fix-its. We expect a quick and easy solution, a quick fix. Maria wanted me, I think, to give her something that would propel her out of bed. Instead, I told her to stay there and to listen to what was going on. Had I tried to fix her, I think it would have prolonged the process of her healing. Instead, I asked her to make her home right where she was.

When a person becomes at home in his or her own shoes it can be a frightening moment. It can also be a moment of great peace and invitation. In order to live our lives fully, in order to grow and develop, we must begin with our feet firmly at home in our shoes. In order to get past depression, loneliness, and a sense of failure—or whatever it is that plagues us—we must learn to stare it straight in the eye. We need to look at our shoes and see not only shoes, but the person who is inside. That is what is meant by the expression that every adversity contains the seed of an equal or greater benefit: Every failure can lead not to more failure, but to success. But we must stare the failure in the eye and see through it in order for that to happen.

My friend the artist J. J. Foley once told me that she does not begin her drawings by drawing. Instead, she spends hours and hours simply staring at the blank canvas, allowing herself to meld with it and allowing images to come. Then she returns to the blank canvas again, this time ready to draw. In the same way, we must stare at the canvas we have before us right now . . . and see through it.

Finding your soul means beginning where you are, with your present worries, cares, joys, and loves, with all of your thoughts, confusions, and morals of the story, and allowing all of that to take you to the world of mystery, the world of God. Yes, the key to finding your soul is to put a *y*—a "why"—into *mastery*, and turn it into *mystery*. Job, in the famous Bible story, endured suffering unequaled by anyone, and had to turn away from the conventional wisdom, which led him to blame others, to blame himself, and to blame God. In the end, he was led to a return of everything he had lost, because he was able to accept the invitation to surrender to the mystery of it all. A sailor has to learn to navigate the seas whatever winds and storms the fates bring him, and in the end to enjoy the process and the wonder of it. A mother has to learn to respond to the endless demands of children as they grow—physical, mental, and emotional and spiritual demands—and to wonder every day at the magic of what lies before her. A radio talk-show host has to learn to field the various calls and the variety of callers on his phones—some nice, some nasty—and to be amazed at the complexity of it all. This is the way of soul. It is what Gabrielle gleaned from years of profound tragedy. It is what Maria is beginning to glean in her grieving.

The place called soul is there for us. Our souls are always watching, always gathering light, always breaking down the superficiality of our daily lives and of our thoughts. We can discover that honey, that light, if we take time to reflect and pay attention.

Chapter Three

Why Me?

Nobody likes to feel like a failure. It's the most unpleasant feeling in the world. How many times I had that feeling when I was in school! I remember sitting in Coach Byard's freshman earth-science class in high school. Pick a day, any day. Dick Byard was a young fellow, on his first teaching job, and was a really excellent teacher. Green he was, but not naive. Besides, he was the football coach, and he was huge, or at least seemed it. By contrast, I was very young, very stupid, and not at all athletic. And I hated earth science. And Mr. Byard liked to call on me.

When I heard the dreaded word "Keenan," all I wanted to do was to slink down in my seat and be anonymous. I wanted nothing more than for the earth whose science I was supposed to be studying to swallow me up and make me invisible. Why me? I wondered. Why couldn't I just be "unchosen" like everybody else? I would have given anything to have been overlooked.

When I stop to think about it, that feeling of Why me? has followed me along, in those times when suffering of some sort or other has found its way into my life. Why me? Why couldn't the teacher call on somebody else? Why am I so diffident when everyone else seems so confident?

The common thread, I think, in these critical and painful situations is the feeling of being isolated. When I cry "Why me?" it is because I feel lost, afraid, without ground to stand on, all alone. The Protestant theologian Paul Tillich explored the modern world and an individual's reactions to its anxieties in a series of sermons titled "The Shaking of the Foundations." That is how we feel when life brings us to a point of crisis. Whether it is the everyday angst of an unprepared schoolkid or the earth-shattering sense of grief and confusion that accompanies a tragic loss, suffering brings with it the feeling of somehow having failed at life, of having failed so badly that we have lost our way altogether. "Why me?" we ask.

Sometimes we deal with suffering by blaming. When something untoward happens to us, we have an almost innate need to get to the heart of it and find someone or something to blame. I once knew an old priest, a very experienced and well-seasoned pastor, who often referred to himself as the Complaint Department. When I asked him why, he told me that the greater part of his time was taken up with parishioners making complaints about something he or someone else did or didn't do.

Often, we blame God. After all, we reason, God is supposed to be omnipotent, and if he can do all things, why doesn't he do something about our situation? It didn't occur to me how often God gets blamed for everything until the day I visited a friend of mine who was in a mental institution. As I entered the building, I met a little boy who couldn't have been more than ten years old. He gave me a rather odd look, obviously eyeing my Roman collar, and followed me as I approached the nurses' station. He came around in front of me and asked if he could speak to me. I asked the nurse, who said yes, and who led us to a small room where we could talk privately. "When I came here," the boy began, "I thought I was God. You know, you have a terrible job when you think you're God." Though I never saw the little boy again, I have often thought of how hard it must be not only to think you're God, but to actually be God.

That little boy was right: God has a difficult job, given the amount of responsibility we try to put on his shoulders. When faced with a tragedy, many of us focus on why God didn't do something to prevent it. When we blame God or blame others for the sorrows and tragedies in our lives, we are trying to cope with the shaking of our foundations. We blame others because we need to have a place to put our suffering. We walk around with the weight of the world and we feel we can't bear it anymore, so we shift it a little by trying to shift the responsibility for what has happened. As a coping device, blaming may be okay in the short run. It can give us a little breathing space while we try to figure out what really happened. But if we always put the blame on others, we end up hurting our relationships and shortchanging ourselves.

As I grow older, I find that I still ask the question "Why me?" when a painful moment comes my way. I do not always know the answer right away. But I have learned that there is an answer, if only I can have the patience to wait it out. Every suffering, I have learned, has a particular gift to give to me; and if I am especially patient, I may find that the gift it is giving me is the gift of living a soulful life. While I am going through the bad days, it often seems to me that good news would be that the painful thing didn't happen after all, or that it was somebody else's fault, maybe God's. But if I allow myself to watch and wait and listen—if I can allow myself to believe that there is something far better and nobler than blaming—I may find that the good news for those bad days is really the gift of awakening to my soul.

To this day, I hate the fact that my friend Maura killed herself. I had met her on the phone one day when I "just happened" to answer the ringing telephone in my parish, and over several months we became friends. She was always a little down, and spoke frankly about her feelings, but it seemed to me that she was really turning her life around. Maura (I have changed her name) had become interested in broadcasting and had been doing some volunteer work for me to help me with my radio program *As You Think.* She had started going to church every Sunday; in fact, the last conversation I had with her was after Mass two days before she died. I was devastated when the superintendent in her building told me that Maura had taken her own life. My first reaction was to blame myself. If only I had been more attentive, if only I had listened more carefully to Maura's conversations, she might be alive today. My route home from one of the radio stations where she and I had done broadcasts took me past the building where she had lived, and I often felt myself filled with sadness and remorse as I passed by.

Knowing how badly I was feeling about Maura's death, people often told me, "Don't blame yourself." I now know that I had to blame myself at least in part for Maura's tragic death. Blaming myself was a sign of how much I cared for her, how much our friendship had come to mean. How could I have thrown up my hands and said, "Well, that was her choice. Too bad!"? I never could. Maura's life and presence in my life had come to mean too much to me.

On the other hand, I did not want to stay trapped in self-pity and self-blame. I came to see that factors other than myself had a part in Maura's decision to die. As time went on, I felt my soul shift a little toward some major realizations. I have often thought of them as gifts from Maura. I learned the importance of listening very carefully to what people in distress are saying, and I learned that I must take it seriously when someone speaks of ending his or her life. But I also learned that, in the final analysis, Maura made her own decision. She had been back and forth on the question of life and death for a long time, and decided it was just too painful to go on living. As I talked to our mutual friends, I was able to realize that I had done a great deal to help her, and that she had made her own decision, one that was tragic, but nonetheless her own. I wish with all my heart that at the moment of her decision, Maura had been able to realize the possibilities that were opening up for her in her life, possibilities for friendships and for a career. Sadly, some darker forces won the day. Those darker forces—her dislike of her job, a devastating personal loss, some family problems— had played a major part in her decision. Dealing with the loss of my friend came to mean coming to define more clearly my own responsibility for her tragic death in the light of other factors in her life. I felt a soulful shift from blaming myself or others or even being angry with Maura herself. My soul was focusing elsewhere, and it was feeling lighter.

As the days and weeks went by, I came to realize that my greater ease of soul was not merely due to my having adjusted to Maura's death or having "moved on." Rather, my soul had begun to ponder deeply the choice that Maura had made, the choice to end her life. I began to wonder what would happen to Maura now. Yes, Maura had done something wrong—she had taken her life. Perhaps I could have done more to help her, but her decision to take her life was ultimately her own. A fundamental rule of life had been broken, and somehow Maura would have to deal with God about that.

On the other hand, if God were to say to me, "What should I do about Maura?" I would reply,

"Be merciful. You know what she suffered and how hard she tried." The light that went on in my soul told me that God knew this even better than I, and he wanted for her the same eternal comfort I did.

The more I allowed my soul to ponder these things, the more I realized that there had to be something beyond condemnation and blaming when it came to God's judgment—the ultimate judgment—of Maura and people like her. I realized that hardness of heart is never a sign of soulfulness, even when it masquerades as moral uprightness. There are people who believe that God applies the moral law with complete strictness, without feeling and without human warmth. There needs to be a moral law: When people like Maura are tempted to commit suicide, for example, they need to know that there is sacredness at the heart of life, and that life provides opportunities and possibilities beyond the apparent darkness of the moment, and that this is a firm rule of life. No matter how much I understood the turmoil that Maura had gone through, in taking her own life she had done something wrong. On the other hand, I came to realize that God rarely if ever applies the law without warmth of heart. Revisiting the Bible, I found a God who patiently waits for his people to return to him, one who is not afraid to lay down the law and to warn them of the worst that can happen, but one who does not hesitate to show them his kindness and his love.

I do not know whether Maura took her life because she gave up on living or because she hoped that God would be merciful and that the next life would be better. I do know that, in dealing with my own sorrow over the choice she had made, I realized that God would find a more fertile ground between condemnation and mercy, a ground of love—and so must I. Maura had been a gift to me in life, and she was a gift to me in death as well. My feelings about her and her death were very personal, it is true. But my feelings had opened a door to a broader, higher, and deeper place within me, where I had come to have my heart touched by the mercy of God. There, in the very depths of my soul, had been born a knowledge that tender and understanding mercy were extended to me, to Maura, and to all of us who suffer in life, and that all we have to do is say yes and accept it. My struggling with the loss of a friend had opened a door to a deeper knowing about myself and all men and women, about God. In death, Maura had softened my heart and led me to a place called soul.

Why me? In some ways, I will never know the answer to that question, and that is fine. But in another sense, I know the answer, and that answer comes from my soul. My suffering opened a door that led to, yes, an appreciation of the moral law, but thankfully also to compassion and understanding and wonder at the miracle of soulful love. When we are able to put aside all of the "coping devices" and allow ourselves to experience what we are truly feeling, we learn that, far from being something that keeps us from making progress, our vulnerability, our suffering, actually opens a door to soulful living. When we allow ourselves to find that place called soul, we begin to see the world with new eyes. Instead of life being full of land mines and monsters, it is seen to be full of messengers who reveal to us our mission to be truly joyous and to make the world a better place. Instead of seeing ourselves condemned to lives of boredom and quiet desperation, we discover what the poet Gerard Manley Hopkins called "the dearest freshness" within ourselves and within our world. Instead of seeing our spouse, our boss, our neighbor as enemies to be blamed for our condition, we begin to meet them with greater understanding and compassion, and allow them to enhance rather than obstruct the mission that we have in the world.

When, in the face of suffering, we ask the question "Why me?" we must remind ourselves that we might just be on the verge of an important discovery about who we are and what we are here for. The soulful guidance that lies deep within us contains an important secret about the destiny and the mission that is ours. Too readily our school systems write off the bored child and fail to see the importance of developing the little genius that is hiding inside. In the workplace, we write off the bored worker, the person who appears to have no interest in anything, and how surprised we are to find that in their off hours, they write poetry or collect art. By the same token, we too readily write ourselves off when the course of our lives has made us feel alienated from the good fortune or success that we imagine others to have. Soulful living means being ready for surprises, and learning to take those surprises not just *with* a grain of salt, but *as* a grain of salt, something that can add zest and interest to our routine lives if only we will allow it.

Allowing ourselves to discover the place called soul—and, more important, allowing ourselves to live there once we discover it—means opening ourselves to a loveliness, a depth, a beauty, a graciousness in life that would otherwise be closed off to us. Who would have known that the shy, dopey kid in high school who hated to have his name called would someday find his calling in life? Certainly not I, and certainly not anyone else with "common sense." Yet here I am. Somehow, my soul insisted on being found, even when I scarcely knew that it existed.

Once we discover the place called soul, we do

not have to feel like failures ever again. No matter how we are viewed in the eyes of the world, we know that there is a mystery lurking inside us that is longing to be expressed. Once we know that, and once we absorb the impact of that truth, our lives and our world begin to change. It is almost as though we begin to inhabit another world even while we continue to live and move in this one. Not that we become neurotic or schizophrenic, for our souls are surprisingly practical and can draw life from the most mundane of situations, but rather we find ourselves drawn to the core of our hearts as we struggle to reconcile the world outside us with the world we are discovering inside.

Chapter Four

The Set of
the Sails

⌇

*T*he place called soul is not in
some other land, in a journey
of a thousand miles, or in
some buried treasure in a far-off place. Your soul
is where you are. The journey that we take to find
our soul is not the same as flying to London or
driving to Indiana. There, we know where we are
going, and we know that where we are going is
truly somewhere else. Finding your soul is different: You find where it is not by going somewhere,

but by being where you are. It is in the midst of your present place that you set your sails.

There is a wonderful story of a poet who stood one day taking in the beauty of the seashore. There was a breeze, and he noticed in the distance a pretty little sailboat being carried by the gusts of wind. At that moment, he noticed a second sailboat moving in the opposite direction. For a time, he was puzzled. He knew the breeze hadn't changed direction. Yet here were two boats being blown in quite opposite directions. How could this be?

The poet thought long and hard until finally he arrived at the answer to his problem. He wrote it in a poem.

> One ship goes east
> The other west
> It's the selfsame winds that blow.
> It's the set of the sails
> And not the gales
> That teach us the way to go.

It's not the way the wind blows in life that makes the difference; it's the way we set our sails in the wind and thus allow the wind to guide and direct us. We can blame the winds for our fortune or misfortune, but it is how we use the wind that makes the difference.

My friend Peter (let's call him) will always be

an inspiration to me. When I began broadcasting, it was at a radio station called IN TOUCH Networks, a national—and now international—radio network for the blind. IN TOUCH broadcasters read magazines and newspapers over the air, free of charge, for visually challenged people, who may tune in with a special radio receiver. During the years I was at IN TOUCH, not only were many of the listeners blind, but many of the engineers were blind as well. Those were the days when the programs were recorded on reel-to-reel tapes rather than the smaller, sleeker, DAT or digital audiotapes, which look like small cassettes. That meant that the engineers had to be able to find blank tapes for recording, find recorded tapes with the right programming for each particular hour, thread the tapes onto the machines, operate the control panel, and cue the broadcasters to start and stop. For a sighted person, that was a lot to do, and I always thought that it must have been daunting for the ones who could not see. All of them performed their duties with capability and tremendous grace.

I came to know Peter exceptionally well. Every morning, Peter would take the subway from Manhattan's Upper West Side down to the studios near Lincoln Center. Often it was cold and dark at five in the morning, and several times Peter was beaten and mugged on his way to work. Never did he let that stop him.

On Saturday mornings, Amy Waxgiser Lloyd and I would broadcast the *New York Times* at seven, live, across the country. Peter would get to work at six to open the station and prepare for the broadcast. As time went by, I would get to the station early, armed with coffee and bagels, and Peter and I would sit in the control room and talk about everything under the sun. I learned that as a young boy, Peter had lived in rural upstate New York with a family who really thought that the best thing to do for a little blind boy was to keep him isolated. Many of us, under such circumstances, would have given in and allowed ourselves to wallow in self-loathing and resentment at how badly life had treated us. We would spend hours bemoaning our fate, and how unfair it was that we have had to be isolated while others have had all the breaks.

Not Peter. Instead of wallowing in rage and self-pity, he set his sails so as to turn the experience of childhood isolation into a dynamic source of energy that propelled him into college. In college, he got involved with radio, which opened his world and created a career opportunity. Somewhere along the way he discovered computers, and he was deeply involved in cyberspace—and this was long before most of us had caught on to the

World Wide Web. And he was very interested and knowledgeable in all forms of music.

What motivated Peter to continue to break through obstacles and barriers and to derive so much enjoyment from life? It was the memory of that blind little boy stuck in the house in upstate New York. Where some would have adapted to a useless life, Peter determined never to let life do that to him again. He blamed no one; he simply determined not to let it happen again.

Had my friend Peter allowed the gales of life to blow him about, he might never have left his childhood home. Peter set his sails for a happy and fulfilled life, and he let the winds blow him in that direction.

For Peter, the journey to his soul took place on the vehicle of the happenings of his life. Indeed, he turned his blindness into a vehicle. Where the vehicle took him was determined by the set of his sails, the attitude with which he gave meaning and direction to his life.

When suffering touches our lives, we can learn to set our sails so that it brings us to a positive direction. We can make it a vehicle for finding our soul.

But what does it mean to set our sails? What can we do in order to turn suffering into growth?

The first step is to realize that it is possible to turn suffering into growth. For many of us, that in itself is a new idea. Many of us learn at a very early age to believe that suffering puts an end to growth.

This is understandable, since that is what appears to be happening when we suffer. Our life is moving along on a particular course and suddenly something comes along that appears to stop it. Life as we have known it seems to be on hold.

When that happens, our first inclination is to escape the suffering, and our second is to fix it. Each of those options is rooted in the all-too-familiar belief that the suffering we are experiencing is "the end of the world." We have to do whatever we can to eliminate the pain and to deal with the disruption in our lives. The fabled Dutch boy who stuck his thumb in the dike and saved the town from flooding knew that what he was doing was not the same as rebuilding the seawall. It was a stopgap measure. All too often, we do not see that our short-term solutions are not a total or final answer.

There may be many reasons for our propensity to take short-term solutions. But chief among them is our belief that suffering, and our present suffering in particular, is a roadblock to the progress of life.

Most people think that the alternative to seeing suffering as the end of progress is to engage in "cockeyed optimism." This attitude holds that when suffering comes along, we can replace it with a positive thought. That works fine for me when stage fright strikes before I start to preach in a packed church, or in the opening moments of a radio broadcast. At such times, a positive thought can help. But a person terrified by the prospect of lifelong paralysis needs more than positive thinking in order to prevail.

There is a third way, different from "suffering is all" and "positive thinking," and that third way is founded in the belief that suffering can be a way to growth. The sails are set against the ill wind in order to make it a part of the longer journey rather than the end of it.

If someone ever asks me for a great lesson I have learned, I will probably say that the greatest lesson I have learned is that failure need not be the end of the road.

Once, on *As You Think*, I had the opportunity of interviewing Steven K. Scott, author of *A Millionaire's Notebook*. At the start of the interview, I asked Steve, "Are you a millionaire?" He answered, "Yes, temporarily." I was stunned and asked him what he meant. "Well," he said, "I'll either lose it here, or lose it when I die."

He then proceeded to tell me about the many failures in his business life: the times he had been fired, the times when he had lost money. I realized as he spoke that the person sitting before me was the same man who had created the phenomenally successful "Where There's a Will, There's an 'A' " infomercials and Richard Simmons's "Deal-A-Meal" videos. One of Steve Scott's secrets for success was learning from failure. Every time he made a mistake, he learned from it and used it as a guide for future practices and procedures. He set his sails so that every failure became a teacher.

The set of the sails is not a positive thought—it is an attitude, a habit, a way of life. What appears in the panic and frustration of the moment to be a permanent setback becomes a door to opportunity.

People often say that they can understand this positive approach to failure and misfortune when it comes to something like losing a business, where you can perhaps start over again. But what about a seemingly irreversible tragedy? What if you are very sick and are about to die? What if you lose a child? What if you watch a loved one lose control over their mind? How can you use failure as a mentor under those circumstances? Is there anything worth learning, or does it matter?

I have always loved Anne Morrow Lindbergh's book *Gift from the Sea*. As she walks the beach, she finds that the sea has washed up shells, rocks, fossils, treasures of all kinds. I have walked the beach a thousand times, looked at the shells, said "Oh, that's nice," and walked on. What makes Anne Morrow Lindbergh soulful is that she looks at those random shells and allows them to be objects of her observation and contemplation.

What if I could do the same thing with the experiences that get washed up onto the beach of my life? What if my life experiences could become teachers and guides toward a deepening of my life? That's what it means to set my sails. What if I set my sails in such a way that, instead of being mere experiences, the stuff of my life revealed to me a mystery and a magic? Setting my sails means going through the daily events of my life expecting to receive guidance, protection, and blessing.

Soulfulness means allowing the everydayness of my life to explode into wonder. Setting the sails means expecting that explosion to happen at any moment. James Allen wrote years ago in his classic *As a Man Thinketh*, "Circumstances do not make a man. They reveal him."

When Joseph Cardinal Bernardin, the beloved Roman Catholic archbishop of Chicago, was dying of cancer, he publicly detailed the progress of his illness and its painful symptoms, and repeatedly used his experiences as a way of teaching others how to live the final days of their lives gracefully. I wonder if I will have that sort of courage when my time comes. Cardinal Bernardin set his sails so as to make the experience of the end of his life as honest and gracious as possible for himself and for others.

In trying to live soulfully, we do not always have a clear sense of the details of where we are going. That's okay. Because if we are watchful, every moment can be a vehicle guiding us in new directions.

To set our sails with the belief that life's vicissitudes are like the winds that blow a sailboat is to believe that those pains and tragedies can actually guide a life. My friend Peter did not allow his blindness and the inconvenience and suffering it caused him to hinder his life, but rather let them define and refine his mission in life and his enjoyment of it. Steve Scott did not allow his failures in business to stop him from being a successful businessman, but rather let them teach him and guide him toward phenomenal success and give him wisdom and depth as well. Cardinal Bernardin allowed the final moments of his life to be a teacher for himself and others. All three men learned how to focus on the present, and how to let it guide them. By staying in the present and learning from it, by allowing their sense of suffering to guide them rather than to lock them into a miserable past or into an uncertain future, they stayed in the moment, no matter how miserable, using it as a guide and finding a gift within it. As we begin to live in the place called soul, we find something intriguing about the set of our sails. As soulfulness becomes less strange to us, we begin to discover that it has been there all along. We may have felt ourselves being blown about by every temptation, every wind of change, every possible misfortune. But as we enter the realm of soul, we begin to see that deep down inside us, there has been a guidance, a depth, a hope.

Imagine what it would be like for a child to stand in front of a mirror and see his or her image as an adult! That is the kind of seeing that soul does. When we were children, our soul was present inside us guiding us to the people, places, and things that would enable us to find and fulfill our destiny, our mission. That is what it means to say that the soul of the child is like a ship whose sails are set on a particular course. Deep within us, there is a knowing about what it is we are to do or become in the world. Our challenge is to listen to the guidance we are receiving and not allow ourselves to be steered on an errant course.

There is a great deal of fascination today with soulful living. That is wonderful. But it must become more than fascination, something that lasts for a few years until we drift off into another set of interests. Finding your soul is not just one among many options in the smorgasbord of life. Being attentive to our souls on a daily basis, doing the things that feed the soul and keep us alive to it, are paramount if we are to be truly happy and to fulfill the purpose for which we are made. We must set our sails every day if we are to stay on course.

Lucky are the people who find their souls as children and who stay on course throughout their lives. Most of us are not like that. Most of us are adults who look into the mirror hoping to find our image as children. In psychology, so much useful work has been done on finding the inner child, which has helped so many people to care for the wounded child within and to release that child so that it can contribute to their life. Soulful reflection adds an important dimension to psychology's approach to the inner child by saying that the divine presence and divine mission of the soul are alive and well during the early years, demanding to be acknowledged and recognized. Finding your soul means looking back in wonder over the course of the past and discovering the mission and the presence that were there all along. Setting our sails as adults often means gazing into the mirror in wonderment and seeing the image of the child, how all along one's character and purpose have been there, waiting to be discovered and released.

Chapter Five

Ambience: What Comes Around Goes Around

I cleaned my apartment last weekend—and this morning I realized it needed cleaning again. You wouldn't think it would be a tough job keeping two small rooms clean. But I was never a neatnik, and with my two beloved cats, Teddy and Flicka, making their long-haired contributions, the place can quickly become a mess.

Ambience means a lot to me. I am sure it is my

mother's influence. Mom was a great housekeeper, who could clean and decorate like nobody else. I never manage to feel that I have achieved a great ambience, but I do try to straighten and decorate so that the place looks at least presentable. I feel better then.

Ambience is a lovely thing for a room to have, and it is also a lovely word to pronounce. I thought that perhaps if I knew what its etymology was, I might have better luck achieving it. When I looked it up, I discovered that its root meaning is "to go around." That's nice. Ambience is what goes around a room. My mind could not resist thinking of the well-worn phrase "What goes around comes around." At that moment, some playful elf inside my head switched the words on me. I found myself thinking, "What comes around goes around."

I sat bolt upright. *That* was the problem with my efforts at tidiness! I bring home so much stuff from the office—books, papers, tapes, you name it— whatever comes around ends up going around the apartment. *All* around it. If I were more careful about what I let in, I would have more control about what went around the apartment, and it would have a nicer ambience. Thank you, elf.

What's true of our rooms is also true of our souls. Once we set our sails so as to find God and guidance on our journey, and once we get our souls unstuck, we have come a long way. But we still need to be careful of what we let in. What comes around goes around. Souls have ambience too. There are cluttered souls just as there are cluttered rooms, tidy souls just as there are tidy rooms. Just as I need to watch what—and who—comes around my room, so I need to watch what comes around my soul if I am to have the ambience I crave. What good is it to get my soul unstuck if I just get it stuck again?

I thought of this again during a casual conversation with a friend. "Lately," she said, "I find myself entertaining the idea of running away. I can't seem to help it."

Something about my friend's turn of phrase hit me like a bolt out of the blue. I couldn't resist.

"What do you serve it?" I said.

A look of absolute bewilderment crossed her face.

"What do I serve what?"

"Your idea," I replied. "You said you were 'entertaining' the idea of running away. I am asking what you serve it. I guess, in a crazy way, I'm asking what you do to make the idea of running away feel at home."

It was a crazy idea. But I was so struck by the fact that my friend had used the metaphor of entertaining. We use it all the time. We entertain thoughts of quitting our jobs, of what we would do if we won the lottery, of running off to a desert island. Sometimes we entertain bad thoughts. But entertain them we do, and we use that metaphor so consistently that we have forgotten what it means.

What we are saying when we speak of entertaining thoughts is that we really want those thoughts to be at home. We are doing something, perhaps unawares, to make those thoughts feel at home. They may really seem to us to be unwanted guests, but if we entertain them, we are allowing them to come back.

When we speak of entertaining thoughts, we are alluding to the notion of our mind as a home. It is not a bad notion at all, because the mind is very much where we live. What we think becomes the atmosphere in which we live and move and have our being. Our lives and the lives of others are lightened or darkened by the thoughts that are in our minds and hearts.

Of course not every idea that comes into our souls is one that we want to welcome. As we grow older, we learn to be discriminating about our ideas, just as we are about our house guests. Ignatius of Loyola, the founder of the Jesuits, told his followers to watch the beginning, the middle, and the end of their thoughts. Often, something that once seemed to be a good idea ends up taking us astray.

As we deepen, we are also led to see that we have a choice to make about the quality of the home or soul we live in. Ideas have consequences. One of those consequences is that our ideas set the atmospheres of our minds and hearts and souls. A soul is a home, and like any other home it has an atmosphere, which is created by those who live there and who are invited to be there. One of the most difficult and important of life's choices is deciding what the quality and ambience of our soul will be.

How many thoughts should we have in our souls? Should we have many or just a few? Should our soul be like a mansion or like a small shack?

Everyone is entitled to build his or her own house and to throw his or her own party. Some people like large parties with hundreds of guests to entertain, while others prefer a quiet evening with a few friends and hate large gatherings. Similarly, some people are happiest when they are reading and thinking broadly and entertaining lots of thoughts and ideas, while others prefer to follow one school of thought or one particular line of thinking. And yet we all want to have more thoughts. Even if we ascribe to one school, all of us love to see nuances and new shades of meaning in our ideas.

The Gospel of John in the New Testament tells a very poignant story. On the eve of his suffering and death, Jesus meets with his disciples to celebrate the Passover. In the course of that evening, seeing how afraid his disciples are of what is about to happen, Jesus consoles them. "Do not let your hearts be troubled or afraid," he tells them. "Trust in God still, and trust in me. There are many mansions in my Father's house."

The expression "There are many mansions in my Father's house" tells the disciples that this is no time to narrow the expansiveness of their souls. Their suffering makes them feel as though they are "out of the loop" of God's favor. In their time of anxiety, Jesus reminds them not to narrow their focus. It is a good reminder for all of us, whether we are Christian or not, religious or not. Times of crisis and suffering do not leave us feeling very expansive. But they are precisely the times when we ought to consider affirming our purpose and strengthening our vision.

My radio program, *As You Think*, has had many crises in its brief history. As a paid program, it relies upon sponsors, listener donations, and fund-raisers to keep going, so that I can pay the station for the use of its time and facilities. There have been times when it appeared we would not have the resources to go on.

On one such occasion, I went to my friend and WOR colleague Joe Franklin, whose *Memory Lane* program has graced the airwaves at WOR Radio for more than four decades. I was pretty discouraged, and I told Joe my tale of woe. He listened very compassionately, and when I had finished he replied, "Father, this is not the time for you to be thinking of quitting. This is the time for you to be thinking of expanding. Think about how many markets you would like to have for *As You Think.*" It was just what I needed to hear. Joe helped me to think in terms of my vision, the vast audience I would like to have for the show. I needed to focus away from the limited vision of my failure and on the expansive vision of success. I needed to entertain not thoughts of failure, but thoughts of expansion.

When we have the entertaining mentality, we do not need to be ruled by any of our thoughts. We are the host, and we are in charge of the house. So if some of our thoughts should become rowdy and obnoxious, we deal with them in the same way we would deal with a rowdy or obnoxious guest.

What can we do when we find ourselves plagued by negative thoughts or becoming negative in general?

We can use strong-arm tactics and try to get rid of the negativity. Bodily throwing out an unwelcome guest sometimes works when we are hosting a party. It seldom works in our minds. The reason is that when we deliberately suppress a thought, we succeed only in focusing our attention upon it. Focusing our attention is the mental equivalent of extending an invitation. To focus our attention upon a negative thought is to let it in. All we have succeeded in doing is increasing our frustration, since at the same time we are trying to eliminate the thought and are inviting it to come in.

There is still another way, and it is probably the

deepest and most soulful of all. At a dinner party where he discovers an uninvited or an obnoxious guest, a host might ask the guest to come to his study and speak to him there in private. He might engage the guest, seeking to determine the nature of the guest's presence and/or attitude. If the guest is uninvited, the host might seek to know how and why the guest entered the party. If the guest is invited but is becoming obnoxious, the host might engage the guest in a discussion of his behavior or his views, and in the end he might either come to an understanding with the guest or might simply tell him to leave. The effect of this approach is to discover the root cause of the guest's presence and behavior.

Something similar might be done with negative thoughts. Instead of putting them away or dealing with them quickly, we might want to take time to listen to what is happening inside us. For example, if we are going through a particular bout with anger, we might take time (either in meditation or in a journal) to address the anger, to ask it how it came, what it is doing here, what it is about. This is the deepest and most soulful approach, for it acknowledges and addresses the anger and it enables the anger to fulfill a purpose in one's life. One of the great surprises of life is learning how the so-called negative emotions we experience can make a contribution to our lives. The fact is, each of these can give us a depth, a passion, a wisdom about life. Dialoguing with our fear can result in our developing a healthy sense of caution. Listening to our anger and addressing it can enable us to develop a passion for life that might otherwise have resulted in frustration. As we address these so-called negative thoughts and feelings, we enable these guests at the dinner party of our mind to bring us a gift. We do not often realize that every guest can bring us a gift if we give it the opportunity to do so.

Being such a gracious and discerning host implies something about the atmosphere of the home—the soul—into which we welcome our guests. It implies that the house is a transforming place and has an atmosphere in which those who enter it are uplifted. Interestingly, this does not always imply that it is neat and tidy. I have gone into homes in which everything was clean and neatly arranged but that had no sense of life in them. By way of contrast, I have been in homes where a lack of perfect tidiness was more than offset by a sense of familial love and warmth.

It is the same with our minds and hearts, with our souls. Sometimes they are a little messy: Our thoughts are random, our feelings are not fully in order. But if our souls are sources of warmth and vitality and life for ourselves and others, we know it and others know it too. Such souls are places where people may come and grow.

Chapter Six

The Teacher Will Appear

❧

I didn't like my sixth-grade teacher at all. Neil Johnston was not the teacher I was ready for, or so I thought. He was a kid fresh out of college, had never taught before, and was as mean as could be, or so I thought. Sister Anne, a lovely Sister who had been our teacher, had been assigned to the eighth grade to fill a vacancy. Studiousness had never been my strong suit. I was one of those kids who really couldn't care less about things like that. At that point in my life, I was interested in listening to the radio and in playing baseball, and that was about it.

All of that changed the day Mother Urban, our principal, came into our classroom with Mr. Johnston in tow. There was no doubt about it, Mr. Johnston was a young teacher trying to prove how mean he could be, and he had it in for me. No longer could I get away with dog-eared assignments and handwriting that smeared its way across the page. His booming voice would make the classroom shake, and me along with it. I hated him.

Mr. Johnston did not return to our school after that year. His first love was music, and I have always imagined that he decided to choose that over elementary school teaching. But those few months of pure hell in which he was my sixth-grade teacher were one of the best gifts God ever gave me.

Mr. Johnston's saving grace was that he loved music. He had been in the chorus of his college, and he loved to sing. He had a resounding baritone voice, and he taught us more about music and singing in those months than most of us get in a lifetime. I can remember his teaching us to sing a tune originally composed for a French peasant dance, and the strains of a Paderewski composition still resound in my ears from time to time. He brought phonograph records from home (no CDs in those days) and had us listen to a wide range of classical music. And I can still hear his resonant baritone rendition of "It's Beginning to Look a Lot Like Christmas."

Mr. Johnston never fully won his battle with me, but he gave me an education in music that changed my life. If there was a single influence in my formative years that led me to love music as I do today, it was Mr. Johnston. In a sense, I was ready for that teacher who, though appearing to be an enemy, gave me a precious gift.

And a bicycle. There was an odd twist to the end of my time with Mr. Johnston. One day, toward the end of the school year, he asked if there was anyone who wanted and didn't have a bicycle. He had an old one at home that he was willing to give away. When he learned I didn't have one, he decided to give it to me. My dad drove me to his house, where he lived with his parents and siblings, and we drove away with Mr. Johnston's old bike. That was the very last I saw or heard of him.

I guess I didn't know that I was ready for Mr. Johnston. With all my heart, I prayed for God to send Sister Anne back into our classroom. But God knew better than that. It was Mr. Johnston I was ready for. I desperately needed the discipline he tried to teach, and my soul longed for the training in music to set it on a course that would last a lifetime.

When I think of Mr. Johnston, I remember the Buddhist expression "When the student is ready, the teacher will appear." We do not always realize that we are ready; on the surface, I was not ready for Mr. Johnston. But somewhere deep down inside, my soul was readier for him than I realized.

Isn't it amazing how many times the people and events that come into our lives are really meant to be gifts to us? Most of us prefer to believe that the events of our lives are coincidental. It just seems easier to say that things happen by coincidence. It relieves us of the burden of having to look for connections among the events in our lives. If we can blame it on luck, or chance, or fate, we have a much easier time of it. But when we live soulfully, we begin to see that things that seem to happen by chance happen for a reason.

When the student is ready, the teacher will appear. That's what the Buddhists say, and that's how it goes with the coincidences in our lives. It seems we have to be ready to be taught, and a number of things need to work together to make that happen. When we are ready, we can learn a great deal about ourselves, our future, and about how to read the signs that are being given to us in the course of our daily lives.

If we are going to live a soulful life, we must learn to see more than meets the eye. People, places, and things that appear to us in our daily lives have more depth than we had imagined them to have, and more of a reason for being there than, on the surface, we would dream of. As we learn to live soulfully, we learn to "seize the day," as the Roman poet Horace said long ago, and see what lies beneath its surface.

When the student is ready, the teacher will appear. There is something in our souls that draws us to the people, places, and things we need. Of course, we are free to choose whether to accept them. Nonetheless, there is something that draws us to those who can best teach us what we need to learn. Coincidental moments, happenstance encounters, are not mere chance events when we live in the world of soul and with the perspective of soul. They are signs along the way, signs of something we are to learn, something we are to do.

Knowing this makes us more alert to the story of life and to the story of God. The adage that "God writes straight with crooked lines" tells us that even the things we believe to be failures and misfortunes may actually contain a lesson or a gift. Every adversity contains the seed of an equal or greater benefit. People such as myself have found themselves flat on their backs in a hospital bed, and through that experience have been reborn.

On a practical level, our disastrous experiences seem like bad breaks. But from the viewpoint of soul, they can be encounters that add immeasurably to the depths of our own hearts and to our appreciation of love and beauty in life.

If you're patient, your teacher will appear—and you'll be readier than you imagine.

Chapter Seven

Dare to Be Ignorant

*O*ne of these days, I am going to teach a course on how to acquire ignorance. Most of the time, I am asked to give speeches on how to fix a marriage, how to build self-esteem, how to pray, how to get through the holidays. Whenever I walk through a bookstore or a library, I am overwhelmed by the amount of knowledge there is in the world. On-line, I look at the various home pages, the curricula of universities, and the collections of libraries throughout the world. There truly is a traffic jam on the information superhigh-way.

But I'd rather teach a course on ignorance. Let others scale the lofty heights of know-how and how-to. When learned professors are giving dis-quisitions on paleontology and rocket science, I will discourse on ignorance.

Some will say that I will be talking about my best subject. Maybe they are right. Some years ago, a friend gave me his copy of a book called *Sin, Liberty and Law*. "You're an expert on sin," he declared. "Here's a book you'll enjoy." By the same token, I am sure there are many who feel that a course in ignorance would be right up my alley.

A course on ignorance, I believe, would be just what the doctor ordered in today's college curricu-lum. In fact, it would be the most useful course anybody could take. Our colleges and universities fill students' heads with all sorts of information on a wide variety of subjects. But how many of them teach young people what to do when they don't know the answers? What do you do when you discover you are ignorant? Our young people, of course, are given the impression that that day will never come; but sooner than they know, there comes the day when they experience a problem or a situation the solution to which they haven't a clue. Our society places so much value on knowl-

edge that it has lost sight of the importance of ignorance.

As a people, we need to learn that one of the
most important things in life is knowing what to
do in the face of sheer ignorance. By ignorance I
do not mean stupidity. I mean ignorance literally:
pure and simple not knowing what to do. For
there are many such times in our lives, and we are
loath to acknowledge them. But unless we face
them, we will continue to be stuck in our suffering. We will continue to go about from place to
place like the biblical camel who races through the
desert in every direction, snorting at every turn of
the wind, seeking the program, the tape, the
course or seminar, the self-help book that will take
us out of our misery.

The fact is, we will never be happy until we
learn to acknowledge that we do not know what to
do. Until we learn to acknowledge that ignorance
can be a virtue, we will never move past the superficial and into the depth of life, no matter how so-
phisticated our knowledge might be. In my own
case, while suffering from a period of profound
depression years ago, I went into therapy, read
every self-help and psychology book I could get
my hands on, learned to keep a journal, took semi-
nars and workshops on the mind. Many of these
were very helpful and gave me a great deal of so-
phisticated knowledge about human nature and

the human mind. It was quite a striking revelation, therefore, to find myself looking within one day and asking, "If I know so much about what it means to be human, why don't I have peace in my heart?" That question jarred me into an appreciation of my own ignorance, and has brought me closer to finding my soul.

Ignorance was brought home to me very dramatically at the time of my father's death. The morning my father died began as a normal Saturday morning. I arose, prayed, and was eating breakfast at a retreat house where I was working when one of the other priests came into the room and told me that I had a telephone call. Before letting me take the call, he told me, "It's your father's pastor in Missouri." That told me everything I needed to know. And it was true. My father had died that morning, of a heart attack, in an airport limousine, in the middle of a conversation, five minutes after leaving his apartment on a trip to San Diego.

I had talked to Dad just a week or so before for his birthday, and he had called on Valentine's Day, two days after that. He was seventy-four, had been in good health; he'd just burst an aneurysm and died. I will always remember that morning as a study in personal shift of horizons, from normalcy and having things under control, to profound chaotic ignorance. During the telephone conversation with Father Thomas, I noticed my feelings hanging as if on a balance. On the one hand, there was the peaceful Saturday morning I had just left, and on the other the awful realization of what was happening. As the priest began to tell me what had just transpired, I felt my feelings shift from my normal Saturday to the realization that my father had had an accident and might be badly hurt, to the realization that his life was over. I began to realize that I did not know what to do, that there were many things to be done, but that I did not know what they were or how to do any of them. I remember feeling the need to delay going back to Missouri as long as possible, as if to try to steel myself against the unknown. I remember feeling physically sick.

What was happening to me? Suffering began and very quickly brought me to the unfamiliar, to a world in which my father was dead and in which I would have to learn to live without him. Before I could get to knowledge as to how to do this, I had to suffer. But more than that, I had to let my suffering move me to a stage of ignorance, a stage in which I had to admit to myself that I did not know how to live, to allow chaos to find its place in my life. Only then could I rebuild on any solid foundation. For me, the solid foundation was a long time coming. For a while, my life was truly chaotic.

I remember the day my father's furniture arrived in a large moving van, and I had to store and dispose of a whole apartment full of furniture and sort through a lifetime of memories in order to do it. I began to experience a creeping exhaustion, both physical and mental, which finally landed me in a hospital and near death, the victim of a faulty thyroid that caused my other major body systems to malfunction. The hospital experience was pivotal for me. As I lay near death in the hospital room, I felt myself surrender and truly relax for the first time in months. But as sick as I was, it was as though I were shedding a heavy burden, one I did not have to carry anymore. Ironically, it was at this very time that the doctors were concerned that I might die. It was as though I had to get past the initial grieving over my father's death, go through a time of literal chaos, and then surrender. But for me, it was more like a state of surrender than one definable moment. I remember going deeply within myself, and knowing—not hoping, not believing, not wishing, but *knowing*—that I was not going to die. That was my movement from ignorance to knowledge. The knowledge I had, the awareness that I was not going to die, began to increase. It enabled me to be interested in my surroundings, to listen to music on the radio, to stay in touch with friends, to enjoy visits.

Almost miraculously, my body began the

process of healing. Medication began to take hold, and after a month I was released to a private infirmary and was back to work six weeks later. Interestingly, the knowing that I was going to live was simply that. It did not tell me what I was going to be doing, or what I was being prepared for, or how long I was going to live. It did not have the scientific specificity of the tests I was undergoing; it did not tell me how or how quickly I was going to get well. It was a knowing that carried with it a lot of ignorance.

The knowing was preceded by a surrender, which was in turn preceded by a lengthy period of chaos. But the surrender was not an out-and-out surrender to the chaos, as though I were waving a white flag and giving in. It was really a surrender to life, and a surrender to an indefinable but very real dimension that lay underneath it. Somehow, I knew that there was life beneath the chaos, something more powerful than what I was experiencing. In essence, I was saying yes to life, the way Dag Hammarskjöld said it in his wonderful memoir, *Markings,* in which he spoke of saying yes to someone, something, somewhere. For me, the experience was a powerful surrender to God. But I do not believe that my profound moment of surrender could have happened without the gift of ignorance.

How scared we are of ignorance, though.

When ignorant, we have the sensation of falling, much as we might have in a dream: of falling, falling, and falling some more, into what appears to be an abyss. In a moment of shock such as I experienced at the death of my father, we are terrified that we might fall forever.

We are also terrified that we might land. In the midst of our falling, we need a guiding, comforting presence, something that gives us permission to fall, and at the same time lets us know that we are accompanied, cared for, and protected.

As it so happened, ignorance had another crisis in store for me. While I was flat on my back in the hospital, the people with whom I was working at the time took it upon themselves to evaluate my performance, in my absence, and to decide that I should reconsider whether I was fit for parish ministry. When I found out, I was angry and devastated, not so much because they were critical of my ministry, but because the evaluation had been done unexpectedly and in my absence during a time of severe illness. I felt betrayed by people whom I had thought were friends while I was well, and who certainly knew and understood how sick I presently was. I felt frustrated: This was absolutely the last thing I needed after losing my parents and while still recovering from a major illness. I knew I was good at my ministry and worked hard at it, and I knew I was loved among the people whom I served.

Looking back on this incident, I realize that it put me on a tightrope. I had to acknowledge my anger, devastation, sense of betrayal, and frustration—all "negative" emotions—without letting them swallow me up and destroy me. Fortunately, I decided that, convalescing or not, I was going to find the strength to move on.

But in a sense I had to give in to ignorance, rather than to the things I knew how to do. I was tempted to report my colleagues to higher authorities. I was tempted to let everybody know how unfair I thought they had been. I was tempted to discredit them in the eyes of others. I was angry and hurt, and there were many times when I was hot to act on my feelings. Luckily, I kept close to that inner voice, which reminded me that living a good life was the best revenge.

The decision to do that helped me to learn how to turn failure into success. I began to pursue a couple of leads for work in other places, neither of which worked, but one of which led to my becoming aware of an opening in a neighboring parish, almost next door to the one in which I had been serving. I spoke with the pastor, told him what was going on, told him that I wasn't sure of my ability to work. Without taking sides one way or the other, he told me he would take me on. And so I was able to tell my former colleagues not only what I thought of their unsolicited recommendations, but that I would be continuing my career in the ministry right under their very noses! For all my bravado, however, I still had a strong sense of failure. I had had the wind knocked out of my sails. I really wasn't sure whether I could do parish ministry again.

Fortunately, the moral is that apparent and inexplicable failure not only can be turned into success, but, better yet, it can actually be an invitation to a transformation of life—if one stays in touch with that inner voice of guidance, and if, while allowing the "negative" feelings to have their say, one does not get sidetracked into a closed and negative stance.

In fact, the next parish not only helped me to reestablish my self-confidence in the ministry, but it also led me to make connections that enabled me to get into broadcasting and to my present work in talk radio, which I so thoroughly enjoy today. I became involved in the work of an organization that coordinated the outreach of the twenty-one Catholic parishes in the area (including, of course, my former parish), and soon became chairman of the board of the organization. That led to my appearing as a guest on *Religion on the Line* one Sunday. After the show, I mentioned to the priest who was the host that I was interested in radio and that if he ever needed a substitute, I would be interested. The following spring, I had a call from Joe Zwilling, the man who would later become my boss at the archdiocese (though he didn't know me personally at the time), asking me if I would like to fill in for the summer as host on *Religion on the Line.* That, in turn, led to my meeting an engineer at the station who encouraged me to develop my own show, which led to my calling a small station in town to see about buying airtime, which led to my meeting Ric Sansone, who would become the producer of my show *As You Think.* Prior to those radio jobs, the pastor at my new parish had encouraged me to take a summer course in broadcasting at New York University, which had enabled me to make a connection at IN TOUCH (a radio network for the blind), where I worked for Carmen Mahiques, an experienced broadcaster who took me under her wing and became my first radio mentor.

Coincidences? Chance events? Not to my mind. Instead they were the direct, though unforeseeable, result of my decision to stay in touch with my inner voice, which was operating precisely when I did not know what to do. If I had folded my tent and given way to the devastation I was feeling, or if I had collapsed into bitterness and the need for revenge, I might not be realizing my lifelong dream of working in broadcasting today.

What I did—and, trust me, I had no idea of the dynamics of this at the time—was to allow my sense of failure and frustration to have its voice, all the while listening to its recommendations without giving in to them. Because I did that, this negative voice was satisfied and continually made way for my deeper voice of inner guidance. When I had the chance to put things together, I realized that I had done the same thing with my illness. Once I stopped fighting it and allowed it its voice, another, deeper, voice was able to be heard, the voice that told me that I wasn't going to die.

There is, then, a knowing beyond what we think we know. When my ministry crisis hit, I didn't know what to do. I wanted revenge, but I wasn't sure whether to give in to that. By looking deep within myself for guidance, I was able to find a place beyond my ignorance, a place that guided me to choices that so very positively changed my life and my world.

Contrary to popular opinion, ignorance is not bliss. Ignorance is panic and pain and helplessness. Yet the essence of true soulfulness, it seems, is to stare failure and disaster in the face and find there the inner resources for triumph over adversity. Magical things can happen when you dare to be ignorant.

Chapter Eight

There Is Magic in Boredom

*B*ack in my early days in New York City, some friends and I took a Dayliner cruise up the Hudson River to Poughkeepsie. The Dayliner is a thing of the past, a fact I very much regret. It was magical, that slow boat ride past West Point and Bear Mountain, past mansions and monasteries and parks, out there in the chill air of autumn. I remember noticing a group of young adults, perhaps in their early thirties, five or six of them, men and women, fellow passengers on the cruise. What fun they were having, laughing, singing, dancing—it was wonderful to watch them, transforming to be around them.

I remember especially the radiant young

brunette who was more or less the leader of the group. You could not help noticing her buoyant laughter, her *joie de vivre*. Her humor kept everyone's spirits soaring; she was the life of the party.

Perhaps that is why, when the boat docked and the passengers were leaving the ship at the end of the day, I was so struck by the blank look on her face. All the joy, all the laughter, had faded, and in their place, as she walked back into the streets of New York, there was a look of dullness, of pain. Her eyes saddened into a metallic gaze. It looked like her heart had frozen over.

What an amazing transformation! The cruise, I guess, had been a time of glorious escape for her. Now everyday life seemed to be setting in again.

While this change was heartbreaking, sometimes we simply suffer from everydayness as truly as we suffer from heartache. Indeed, boredom is a part of life's suffering that often goes unnoticed, although it is no less significant than more palpable pain. We have all known boredom. We have all lost interest in life at one time or another. In fact, the word *interest* comes from the Latin words *inter* and *esse*, meaning "to be between" or "to be among." I am interested in something when there is a link between that thing and myself. I am bored when that link is absent.

Years ago, my friend the late Father John Lyons from Rockhurst College told a story about a little girl who accompanied her mother to church. When the preacher got up in the pulpit to begin the sermon, the mother noticed that her daughter had begun to sit with her head back and her eyes fixed on the ceiling. This went on for quite some time, until finally the mother couldn't stand it any longer and asked the little girl, "Darling, why are you looking at the ceiling? Why don't you look at the preacher instead?"

"Oh, Mommy," the daughter replied, "I'm watching all those big words go sailing over my head!"

All of us preachers hope that the little girl's experience is the exception rather than the rule. But it's a great story, because it tells us much about interest and boredom. The little girl sensed no connection between the preacher's words and herself. She was not interested, in the literal sense of the word. She was bored with the sermon, and became interested in the ceiling instead.

When we are interested, there is a connection between ourselves and something else. If something is interesting, it links or connects us. And it does that by drawing our attention.

Attention is the means our soul uses to link us to people and places and things that interest us. The word *attention* comes from Latin words meaning "to stretch to." Attention is what happens when our soul stretches to link us to someone or something beyond ourselves.

When something is interesting, it stretches us, and we speak of "expanding" our consciousness, and increasing our attention "span." When we suffer, the flow of life can become blocked.

Suffering can take the edge off of life and eventually make it seem dull and uninteresting to us. When people suffer for a very long time, they can come to feel that life is passing them by. Stephanie Ericksson, author of *Companion through the Darkness,* told me that after her young husband had died unexpectedly, she felt isolated from the events of her life and from her friends. She remarked how often, after a loss, we come to realize that some of our friends isolate themselves from us. They are awkward around us and do not know what to do. When that happens, we, the bereaved, can feel that their isolation is due to something we have done. Often it becomes difficult for us to reach out to others, to socialize, without feeling like personal representatives of the Grim Reaper. There are moments in the grieving process when we want and need that isolation, but there are times when we need the company of people. Given too little isolation, we lose the opportunity to grieve. Given too much, we become depressed and feel separated from the flow of life. Our souls can become frozen, and if this goes on long enough, we lose interest and become bored with life.

There is so much boredom in the world because people by and large have become indifferent to the depth in their lives and their surroundings: There is too much suffering, it takes too much effort to accomplish too little. Life has become so overwhelming. In turn, boredom and indifference breed lack of attention. Who has time, we say, or the energy, for details?

"To know when one's self is interested," wrote Walter Pater in his *Marius the Epicurean,* "is the first condition of interesting other people." When we are interested in something, we are fully engaged, fully alive to what we are experiencing. On the other hand, there is nothing worse than having to pretend to be interested in something, or in pretending to be interested in life when we are not. But what can we do when we find ourselves bored, not interested in anything that we find around us?

The first thing might well be to sit for a while with our boredom. The feeling of being bored has two dimensions. On the one hand, it contains an invitation to slow down, to stop what we are doing. On the other hand, boredom contains within itself a restlessness, a desire to move on, even though we do not know what direction to go in.

Normally, at first, we yield to the restlessness. How many times as children did we say to our mothers, "I'm bored. There's nothing to do." Our mothers, correctly, pointed out to us the hundreds of things that were available to us. Sometimes they would sneak in an agenda of their own: "If you really want something to do, clean up your room!" In any event, the usual way of dealing with boredom is to look for activities to occupy us, to distract us.

We do that even as adults. One of the reasons, I think, that so many people give in to needless consumption is to relieve themselves from boredom. They have become bored with the familiar, and long for something new.

There is another way of dealing with restlessness. Rather than give in to the restlessness inherent in our boredom, we might consider giving our boredom its voice. One way of looking at boredom is to see it as an invitation to slow down, to take some time away from the welter of things that have lost their novelty and have made life lose its luster. Viewed in this way, boredom is an invitation to say good-bye even when we are not yet ready to say hello to anything in particular. We become chronically bored when we do not accept the invitation to say good-bye to old ways of doing things. We can see this only if we allow our boredom to speak to us.

The importance of the good-byes and hellos in life was brought home dramatically to me in a sermon given by Dr. Robert Schuller during one of his televised services from his Crystal Cathedral. He spoke of how we are constantly invited to say good-bye to one phase of life and hello to another. We say good-bye to the womb and hello to the world, good-bye to infancy and hello to childhood, and so on, all through our lives. Dr. Schuller pointed out that it often puzzles people to think of "good-byes and hellos." We think it is a mistake: "Don't you mean 'hello and good-bye'?" we ask. But our experience, he pointed out, tells us that we must say the good-byes before we can say the hellos.

When I heard that sermon, I realized how right Dr. Schuller was. We would like to be able to say hello before saying good-bye, but in fact one of the reasons that we often don't get to say the hellos we want to say is that we haven't yet said the good-byes we need to say.

When we stop to listen to our boredom, we find that it signals us that it is time to say good-bye to something in our lives. This is especially true of our relationships. Romantic relationships begin in the glow of love, but after a while the presence of each other becomes routine, and the glow gets lost in the hustle and bustle of everyday life. When this happens, relationships often become rocky. Arguments increase, though usually the arguments are not really about money, the housekeeping, hobbies, and so on, as they appear to be. Deep down, an important source of the arguments is frustration and disappointment at the state of the relationship itself. The problem with dullness is that it creeps up so gradually that it is often the last thing to be noticed. And so we argue more than we should, or we spend time doing things or buying things and eventually end up doing things separately, pursuing separate interests. However, if the boredom is faced and addressed, it can actually become a doorway to a deeper and more intimate way of relating. As we say good-bye to ways of relating that we don't want, we can say hello to a rich and soulful marriage.

From time to time, I think of that young woman on the Dayliner cruise. Did her metallic gaze eventually open the door for her to find true joy and beauty in her life, or did it leave her dull and downcast? I pray that she has found the happiness for which she has such an obvious talent. I pray, too, for myself and for all of us, that we may come to know that there is, in fact, some magic in boredom.

Chapter Nine

You Call This Work?

*I*n 1997, as my radio program *As You Think* was close to celebrating its fifth anniversary on the air, with the help of my friend Joe Sano I put together our first annual Citizens of Merit dinner at Tavern on the Green. Some 250 people gathered at that prestigious Central Park restaurant to honor prominent people who were making a positive difference in the world. Joe Franklin, veteran broadcaster on radio and television, has welcomed thousands of celebrities and lesser luminaries to his programs and made each of them feel like the most important person in the world. Dr. Irene Impellizzeri, vice president of the Board of Education of New York City, has long provided a strong, loving, and courageous presence to the education of youngsters in the city. Dr. William Donohue, president of the Catholic League for Religious and Civil Rights, is an outspoken advocate for Catholics and others who have been persecuted for the practice of their religion. Frank Ruta, an executive in Manhattan's Garment District, is a leader in the business community who inspires his colleagues and business associates to be positive and industrious in their work. Police Officer Steven McDonald, his wife Patti Ann, and son Conor are a family who shows remarkable courage not only in the way they have faced Steven's paralyzing injury in the line of duty, but in the way they have encouraged and inspired others by word and example.

We decided to honor these people as Citizens of Merit because of the way they inspire others. After the dinner, when I had an opportunity to reflect on the event, it occurred to me that there was something else very special about each of them. Every one of our Citizens of Merit absolutely loves his or her work. Each of them treats his or her work as not only a job, but as a profession, a deeply pleasurable way of making a positive contribution to society. I honestly hadn't thought much about it before the dinner, but now it struck me forcefully: These men and women are so dedicated because they love what they are doing.

When you love what you do and do what you love, it makes all the difference in the world. I know: I love being a priest, and I love being a talk-show host. You can work long hours, get really tired, and yet feel so good just doing it. Is it work or is it play? Who knows?

Not everyone is so fortunate. Not everyone loves their job. Quite the contrary. Yet each one of us has something that he or she loves beyond all telling. It may be your golf game. It may be reading for the blind. It may be saving lives as a volunteer firefighter. A friend of mine occasionally talks about going to Australia to help the volunteers who care for injured koala bears. Whether we love our job or not, part of soulful living is finding what it is we love and making time to do it.

When we do what we love, it seems to me we are less preoccupied with what we have and do not have. Getting what we want is probably the thing most people think about and focus on more than anything else. We plan and work; we sweat and strain. Though we try not to, we envy those who seem to have accomplished more than we. Sometimes when we get what we want, we can't allow ourselves to appreciate it.

The question of pleasure and the realization of

our desires is one of the most critical ones surrounding the issue of living a soulful life. The decision to live soulfully puts an entirely different spin on the nature of our desires and how to fulfill them. When we live soulfully, doing what we love at least some of the time, we see life in a different way, and the difference changes both what we desire and how we go about getting what we want.

You mean it's okay to pursue pleasure, to follow the desires of our hearts? If you think about it, it seems strange that we ask the question as often and as intensely as we do. For what else is there to pursue? It is natural for us to want things; when we want things, it is pleasure that we want. So why do we fret so much about wanting pleasure? It seems as if the answer to our question is affirmative: It is fine and natural to pursue pleasure.

This answer, while true, is incomplete. Much of the advertising that we see and hear seems to tell us that pleasure is pleasure and that is that. "Don't think about anything else," the ads seem to tell us. "Think about this car, this appliance, this dream vacation. Pursue this. Don't think about anything else." So we spend, we get in over our heads, we sacrifice someone else's needs for the sake of the object of our desire. Anyone who has become financially troubled due to the misuse of credit cards knows what I am talking about. Where did pleasure go? It was there when we started out, and it was there for a while after we got what we wanted. But where is it now?

It doesn't take long before we find that pleasure always has a context, and that context has to do with our values. If my buying the expensive new car I saw in the ads means putting myself into irretrievable debt or risking my ability to put food on my family's table or to pay for my children's education, there is a problem. The time comes when we must learn that pleasure fades when the object of our desire conflicts with the pleasure of fulfilling other and deeper needs. Granted, there is nothing wrong with the pleasure involved in having a flashy new car. But there is something wrong when I ruin my life over it or jeopardize the well-being of others in order to have it. As we mature, we learn that the fulfillment of pleasure must be guided by a hierarchy of values, and when it is not, then the piper must be paid.

The answer to the question "Is it okay to pursue pleasure?" then, is yes and no. If we are to live happy lives, we cannot blindly pursue one pleasure after another. As we mature—as we live a soulful life—we begin to realize that there is more to the business of pleasure than we had suspected. Pleasure does not come just from things themselves, as we had thought. Pleasure comes from something within us, from an ability to order our lives. When we find what we love to do and give ourselves the time to do it, we are less likely to try to satisfy every whim. Our lives are focused, and we make choices in a more centered way.

In our highly materialistic society, it is easy for us to be wooed by the prospect of owning a lot of things. A woman told me that somehow she felt her marriage was happier in the days when she and her husband were poor. Now they had ample means, and she appreciated the freedom that the money had given them. But somehow, she felt, the money had created a burden that had drained the life from their marriage. I knew what she meant. I think my happiest Christmases with my parents were the early ones when they did not have a great deal of money, but went out of their way to make Christmas special. Each Christmas, out of the box would come homemade decorations: a pair of white plastic horses, Bill and Nell, with red and green ribbons around their necks; a pair of glassine angels that graced the heights of the tree; a glittery cardboard star that sat proudly at treetop; and a manger that my father made from two-by-fours. Christmas in later, more prosperous years was wonderful, but never quite so special. There are deeper pleasures than those embedded in material objects, no matter how wonderful they be. Part of living soulfully is realizing when we are letting ourselves be lured away from our true focus and instead are focusing on things that are peripheral.

Pleasure that is truly soulful seems to point to

something beyond itself, in the ability to order our lives. It seems to point to something within.

We were made for something beyond the limits of our ordinary experience. The soulfulness we are made for, itself beyond our limits, transforms our limited realities and suffuses them with a graciousness. As we learn to live soulfully, the pleasure we take in external goods changes from a self-centered preoccupation with our own immediate good and begins to take into consideration the good of others as well. Pleasure in our thoughts and ideas changes them from a dry accumulation of facts and information into the joy of knowing. Pleasure in giving takes our focus beyond the material thing we are giving, toward the love and appreciation that our gift is meant to express. At Christmastime, I recall, my father would often purchase a beautiful piece of jewelry for my mother. His pleasure was not in having it, but in giving it to her and seeing her appreciation. Hers was in feeling the love expressed in the gift.

Experiencing pleasure in these ways means fulfilling your heart's desire. It means living a soulful life.

How do we know what to desire? How do we find the desire of our heart? That's a tough question, yet one we face all the time. Are we condemned to freedom, as the existentialist philosopher Jean-Paul Sartre once claimed? After all, if everything points to something else, how can we ever hope to find what we want? I am astonished to think that not so many years ago, I felt my life was utterly insignificant. It amazes me to think what a few short years have done. The difference, I know, has a lot to do with the seriousness with which I have learned to treat my soul.

How can we know what we want? In general, I think we begin by at least tacitly agreeing to take care of our souls. Once we do that, we begin to find our wishes, and as we do that, we begin to find which wishes we want to manifest. The amazing thing is that once mere wishes become desires, we almost cannot stop the process from having a life of its own and leading us step by step.

I am not a career counselor, and when I need one or when someone else does, I have people I can turn to who are experts in career counseling and in personnel. But if someone came to me not knowing what they wanted but knowing that they wanted to change their lives in some way, my first advice would be to take care of their souls. We all know the expression "If you have your health, you have everything." I would change that to "If you have your soul, you have everything." For it is the soul that provides the home, the atmosphere, the context within which the needs of life and the struggles of life can be resolved.

Taking care of the soul means different things at different times in our lives. Last year I went on vacation and stayed for two weeks in a small suburban house in Mississippi, near the Gulf of Mexico. The house was warm and cozy, and I found myself surrounded by lovely trees, beautiful sunrises, and the sweet sound of a baby cardinal who sang all day long as he flew from tree to tree. I realized how much I longed for this quiet life in nature, and how neglecting that had caused me to become tense and irritable and down in recent weeks. In other words, I learned that one aspect of taking care of my soul just then meant making sure I had enough time to relax and enjoy the beauty of nature.

Instead of rushing to read the want ads when we find ourselves at a crossroads in our lives, we need to take time to care for our souls, to make sure that the deepest part of us is getting what it needs. If we find ourselves longing for gardens, we need to do a little gardening within our souls instead of rushing to the next office job. Who knows where it might lead?

Ask a priest who in midlife went to broadcasting school.

When we are stuck in a crossroads and are wondering "What do I desire?" a good place to look is to the things we love to do. Many times we assume that we could never spend our lives doing the thing we love. Experience or some voice in our heads has told us that doing what we love cannot possibly be a career option. When we start thinking differently and thinking seriously about doing what we love, it's amazing what leads our souls provide us.

Once, when I was having an art show catered, I asked the caterer how she had come to start her own business. She told me that she had done it out of necessity, when a personal tragedy in her life had made it necessary for her to find employment. She liked food and liked to cook, so she took it from there. A friend who is a speech coach came to New York as a young woman aspiring to be an actress. She went to a coach for speech lessons. They fell in love and married, and she was his partner in the business until he died. For forty years, she has coached on her own, and many celebrities owe the success of their careers to Liz Dixon's diligent training.

I happen to love animals and have a way with them. I have two wonderful cats, and seem to have a special gift for understanding cats and dogs. Someone once suggested that I might spend my life taking care of animals. I doubt that I shall ever do that, but it is just the sort of soulful lead that someone with a similar leaning might take up and serendipitously launch a career.

If you want a new direction for your life, ask yourself, "Is there anything I am *really* interested in? What do I love to do?" Often that's enough for a wonderful new start.

Living a life of attention to the soul is a very adventurous way to live. It forces us beyond the normal categories and boundaries of everyday thought about life and possessions and careers. Some people find this adventure delightful. Others are frightened by it. They feel that it is too undisciplined, too helter-skelter. The fact is, soulful living requires careful discipline. Soulful living is not to be confused with following every breath of wind that blows one's way; the soul has its purposes and asks us to pay careful attention to them. My work in broadcasting, though deeply soulful, requires a lot of effort, and at times involves discouragement and disappointment. A friend whose wife is a pediatric cardiologist often tells me about the long hours and tiring schedule that make up her life. Soulful living means doing the work of the soul even when one does not feel like it. As a college student, I devoured a book called *A Student's Guide to Intellectual Life*, by a French scholar, Jean Guitton. One chapter of this little book was called "Working while Tired or Sick." In it, Guitton advised young scholars to resist the temptation to cease working when they fell ill or were fatigued. He advised doing different kinds of work, perhaps reviewing or revising, during those down times, but not quitting. The soul needs to be doing its work even in times of rest.

In fact, the soul works in the background even when we are not paying particular attention to it. Computer users are familiar with this concept. Sometimes, when I am writing and using my word processor, I have a crossword puzzle running in the background. Both programs are running at the same time and I can bring the puzzle into the foreground if I need a break or get an inspiration about a clue. We may be busy about our work and not really thinking about our soul, but it is there in the background nonetheless, watching and guiding.

How hard do we have to work at achieving our desires when we live soulfully?

It's a complex question. There are writers on spirituality who claim that when we live soulfully, we easily and effortlessly manifest the desires of our hearts. They claim that there is no longer any need to set goals or to strain ourselves at working to achieve things. If we are attuned to our souls, they say, the things we want can happen instantaneously.

There is a truth, I believe, to what they are saying. Soulful living opens us up to the surprising nature of our lives. Our souls present us with leads as to what to do and where to go, and staying attuned to the soulfulness of our lives provides us with an active and ongoing guidance that is quite remarkable. When we do our soul-directed work, we find that the soul provides for us in ways that we could not anticipate on our own. An idea will come from nowhere, a long-forgotten memory will suddenly stop by to illustrate a point we were making. When I worry and strain about money, I am painfully aware of how little there is, but when I relax and release my needs to my soul, the soul leads me to the money I need. I always remember the night the money for a broadcast showed up unexpectedly just minutes before the show began. It happens. The vacation in the house in Mississippi, I know, was the result of soulful thinking months before about how someday I would like to live in the country and how I would like to spend some time that summer trying it out to see if I liked it. I had no idea how or whether it would happen. I just put the idea into my soul and let my soul work out the details.

It is much easier to work with the soul than to try to struggle on one's own. Working soulfully, we work and achieve more easily and effortlessly as we follow the soul's energy and guidance. But at the same time it is work, and demands both persistence and dedication.

The key to living and working soulfully is surrender. As you develop a sense of your soul and its ways, you learn the importance of surrender. In Old Testament times, God told his people, "My thoughts are not your thoughts, nor my ways your ways." Soulful living requires humility, but it is the only way to lasting joy, to happiness in the long run.

Indeed, the realization of our desires takes work, but it is a different kind of work when it is soulful. Our ordinary way of working is to work ourselves to the point of frustration and exhaustion. When we work in unison with our souls, that spark of the divine within us, we may still work long hours, but our work will have a grace and an ease about it that will give it a prayerlike quality. The medieval monks had a motto: *Laborare est orare*, meaning "To work is to pray." That's what happens when our work has a soulful quality. The work itself may have the air of drudgery to it, but doing that work can be a profound experience of union with God. An old poem from the metaphysical period of poetry says, "To sweep a room as for Thy (God's) laws/Makes that and th'action fine." I am reminded of my mother, who told me that she loved her Tuesday ironing days because they gave her a chance to think.

Living soulfully does not always mean doing work we love. My mother didn't especially love ironing. How can we have this experience of soulfulness while doing a job that is not agreeable to us? The secret lies in separating the outer work and the inner soul. My mother had the right idea: The tedium of ironing was offset by the inner work of thinking. In *The World's Religions*, Huston Smith tells of a branch of Hinduism in which the spirituality of work centers upon the ability to make just this kind of separation. "Identifying with the Eternal," he writes, "the worker works; but as the deeds are being performed by the empirical self, the True Self has nothing to do with them." We can do this, Hinduism teaches, by detaching ourselves from the consequences of our actions. Perhaps I am doing my job only in order to make the money that allows me to do something that I truly love. The interesting thing about this method is that often enough, the results come more easily and effortlessly than if we worried about them. The soul knows how to direct us, if given half a chance.

Learning to live soulfully, we find ourselves becoming different persons with a different approach to life. We find ourselves not exactly living in the same world as many of the people around us. Where they are tense and irritable and anxious over the limitations of worldly goods and their lack of energy and time to achieve them, soulful people are confident in the abundance of life, and are constantly amazed by the ways in which life unfolds. Instead of focusing on lack, soulful people are in awe of the abundance of the world, at the myriad ways God presents himself to them. They have a confidence that is not the "self-confidence" of citizens of this world but rather a confidence in the divine directions of life. Where others struggle and strain to overcome the limitations of their experience, soulful people work hard and work smart all at once, for they know how to draw inspiration from their endeavors.

Can we live a life we love? Is it okay to take pleasure in our lives? Soul says yes and invites us to follow its guidance to a life of vision and purpose. "You call this work?" others may ask us. We smile, knowing that the real name for what we do is love.

Chapter Ten

Stop, Look, and Listen

*G*ood news is always welcome, but on bad days it is something we truly yearn for. It is then that we begin to ask deeper questions and to look for reasons, answers, solutions to life's problems. If things get desperate enough, we carve out some time for reevaluation and reflection. We make the inward journey to explore the various places of our soul—those feelings, attitudes, beliefs, memories, and experiences that make up our inner life.

One of life's downturns that we hear a great deal

about these days is the "midlife crisis." More and more, I hear people talking about it. Most of us try to treat it lightly, to make a joke of it, hoping it will go away. But it does not go away. It is like a bloodhound pursuing us from behind. We try to run, hoping to hide. But it is there nonetheless.

When I had my fiftieth birthday, I decided that the thing I wanted most of all was to celebrate the day with friends. My friends came together and we had a magnificent party with wonderful food and entertainment. Part of the humor was the presence of black balloons, statues of black cats on the tables, black napkins. Today I received in the mail an invitation to the fiftieth birthday party of a friend. The envelope and card are all in black, and my friend is described as being "about to travel across the boundary of Mid-Life." Several months after my own fiftieth, another friend advised me that it wasn't the fiftieth birthday that was the hard one, it was the fifty-first. As we approach or pass "the Big Five-0," we think of death. We try to cover it up, we try to make a joke of it, but it is clear that we are crossing a threshold. It is a passage that makes us stop and think.

For a while I found it difficult to relate to the notion of midlife crisis. For me, the months since fifty have been very happy and productive months. I have not spent a great deal of time thinking about death and the years ahead, and there has certainly been no morbid preoccupation with them. But I must admit I think more about decline and death than ever before. I find myself looking at the obituaries a little more often, marveling at the ages of the people who are there. I have joked about being relieved to open to the obituary page each day and to find that my name is not there. It nearly happened to me once, and it was a real shock. I was reading an article in our diocesan Catholic newspaper, *Catholic New York*, about a lecture I had given somewhere when my eyes hit the headline in the next column: FATHER KEEGAN DIES. The similarity of the names was a little too close for comfort. I laughed, but I was startled as well.

The midlife crisis and its concomitant sense of mortality come earlier for some than for others. I know people who are traumatized about hitting forty, and others who have given very little thought to turning eighty. Not everyone has a midlife crisis, but I think most of us do. It is a time when we sense our limits. Can it be a time for truly living soulfully?

There is no universal midlife crisis, no one-size-fits-all. Each of us goes through it in a very individual way. Some people experience a strong fear of death; having experienced so profoundly my parents' very peaceful deaths, and having been at death's door once myself, I do not. I am as likely to protect myself against an oncoming car as anyone, but I do not go about my day in mortal fear of dying. Some people do. The very fact that they cross the threshold of forty or fifty seems to make them palpably afraid of meeting the Grim Reaper at any second. I like it here, but I tend to have more of a sense of excitement about experiencing a new life and of undertaking a new mission there, which is how I view the afterlife. When others spoke about their midlife crises, I began to muse that while I had had my share of crises, none of them seemed to have been about being at the midpoint of life.

One Saturday night on my radio program, *As You Think,* I decided to try to broach the subject of midlife crisis. Rather than trying to sound like the expert I wasn't, I told my audience very candidly that I needed their help in trying to understand what midlife crisis was, that I kept hearing about it but didn't know very much about it. Luckily, I had introduced other topics that evening, because the only call I received on midlife crisis was from a woman who scolded me for being so ignorant! "I simply don't understand how someone of your background and experience could not know about midlife crisis," she said. When I pressed her, she didn't have that much to offer on the subject herself. As a result of her call, I wasn't that much more knowledgeable than I had been before—and I felt even more stupid than I had initially.

My friend Martina's phone call to my office,

later in the week, gave me better information. We had spoken a few days earlier about a medical condition that she was experiencing. I was dismayed when I had heard that she might be sick again, because she had been through serious surgery for a life-threatening condition just months before, and had just gotten back on her feet, looking, feeling, and sounding wonderful. Now she was calling me to tell me that, at the suggestion of a friend, she had gone to a physician who practiced alternative medicine, and that, though she was skeptical, she thought there might be something there for her.

I was amazed to think of this latest turn of events in my friend's life. The last several years could be described only as tumultuous ones. Although Martina was an extremely happy and vivacious person, she had gone through a period of deep soul-searching following the loss of her mother several years before. An only child, she felt terribly alone after her mother's death, and though she and her husband are profoundly in love in a wonderful marriage, she found herself longing for and missing the relationship she had experienced with her mother.

Several other traumatic experiences ensued during this period. A creative project to which she had given her heart and soul, though beautifully executed, was not as successful as she had hoped, and her efforts to publicize and revive the project seemed to go nowhere. This led her into a deep sense of disappointment and to pondering whether she should undertake further projects. "What's the use," she would say, "if nobody finds out about them? Why bother?"

At about the same time, Martina and her husband underwent a nerve-racking living situation when the construction of a restaurant and the ensuing late-night noise once the restaurant was completed made it impossible for them to sleep. At length, they decided to look for another apartment, a process that proved to be as discouraging as it was tedious. At last they found one they liked, got packed up, and moved their boxes into it. No sooner were they there, their belongings still in boxes, than Martina learned that she was seriously ill and had to undergo major surgery. She recovered beautifully, and was finally able to unpack her boxes and to truly live in her new home. Now she had discovered the problem that brought her to the alternative doctor and to further medical tests.

I said to Martina, "You know, this is uncanny. I have been wondering about midlife crisis, and here you are, calling me today. What do you make of all that has happened to you?"

"For me," she replied, "the most jarring thing about all of this has been a change in my sense of the thrust of life. For a long time, I was kind of sailing through life. I did my job, got married to someone whom I had loved deeply for a long time and still do. Life couldn't have been better. Now it seems more like I am being pushed through life. I keep getting thrust into situations I would not choose to be in, really difficult moments. I don't know why I am being pushed into these moments, these situations. I have the sense that somehow, at this point, my life should be better than it is. Why does everything have to be so hard?"

"Perhaps," I said, "you're being led into something, and every step you are going through is a stepping-stone to that new vista."

"Well, that could be," she mused. "Because the funny thing is that, through all of this, I have the incredible sense of being guided, of being protected. When I went to the alternative doctor I was really out of my league. Yet I had the sense that everything was moving me to go to him, that I was being guided to go, and that nothing bad would happen to me."

As Martina and I talked, I had the sense that perhaps I knew more about midlife crisis than I had imagined. In my own life, I, too, had had a sense of sailing along, getting things on course, and then having everything go awry. I just had not associated it with midlife. During my twenties and thirties, it seemed like every year was a turbulent year, especially in comparison with the fairly simple years of my childhood and adolescence. Religion and soci-

ety were going through a tremendous upheaval—
these were the '60s and '70s—and it seemed that
every day either my seminary training in the Jesuits
or simply life itself challenged the sacred and simple
beliefs that I had carried through my college years.
Though quiet and diffident, I had a great deal of
certainty about who I was during my college years.
That changed drastically and painfully. In those
days, the seminary walls had expanded greatly and
exposed me to a great deal more of life than I had
seen before, with larger ideas, not all of them ortho-
dox, about the role of priests, about the nature of
God, about what was morally right and wrong,
about authority in the Church and in society. Especially in the earlier years of seminary, I found myself
wrestling with my own concerns about whether to
be celibate or married, whether to be a scholar or
more "socially minded." If it was a painful time for
me, I think it was painful for my superiors as well.
In my first year of theology (the final period of
preparation before ordination), I left the seminary I
had been attending and returned to teaching for a
few months. One of the things that compelled me
to do that was a statement made by the dean of the
seminary to the first-year students shortly after we
arrived. "We don't know what theology is," he told
us. "We don't know what priesthood is. So my advice to you is to dig your own trench and stay out of
mine." It seemed to me that if that Jesuit seminary

didn't know what priesthood was, it was no place for me. I understood the dean's pain, however; it was a confusing time, and it was difficult for those in positions of leadership. By the grace of God, I found another seminary and completed my studies and was ordained. Even then, my soul was restless. I was happy being a priest, but I never seemed to fit in with things. The most serious conflict surrounded my getting a doctorate: My parents and my Jesuit superiors really insisted that I do that and become an academic, something I would have died for years ago. Now, for some reason, I was completely uncomfortable with all of that. Having been through so many years of studies, I just wanted to give back something of myself; I didn't want to take more time out for more studies that I wasn't sure I was really interested in. Finally, I gave in and entered a graduate program at Fordham University. As things worked out, I did not finish the doctorate. But strangely, had I followed my own wish and not gone to New York, I would never have met Cardinal O'Connor or the New York Archdiocese and found a happiness, acceptance, and peace that I could only have dreamed about when I was a Jesuit. Perhaps I would never have discovered opportunities in radio.

So when Martina talked about being pushed through life, being in pain but being guided, I understood completely what she meant. Because I, too, know that I have been guided by my soul all the way along. My soul seems to have known where to go, even when my conscious mind was in pain and turmoil. Once I began doing *As You Think* and began to notice the positive and inspirational directions my spirituality was taking, I began to notice keenly that I was being guided, that the odd and often troubled pieces of my life had led me to something exciting and wonderful and deeply soulful. My life is not over yet, and I do not know what the ups and downs of the rest of my life will be. I do know that I can trust that inner guidance. It has worked until now. To me, it is the presence and the guidance of God.

So when I read in the Scriptures about God leading his people out of captivity, luring them out of their complacency, cajoling them when they sidetracked themselves into believing things to be divine that were not and when they missed the messages that were truly of God, I feel that I am reading the story of my life. Just as James Hillman in his enticing book *The Soul's Code* speaks of the soul being like an acorn that in a determined manner marches itself along until it gives rise to an oak, so I believe my soul has been marching me along with determination to the point where I am now, that it will march Martina along in her new directions, and that it will do the same for anyone who sincerely stops, looks, and listens to the guiding voice of soul throughout his or her life. "Even though I walk through the Valley of Darkness, I fear no evil," the Psalmist says, "for you are at my side." How did the Psalmist know, so many centuries before me, how to tell the story of my life?

For Martina, for me, for all of us, the secret is something that we learned in our early years of grade school. For me, it was in the first grade, and I can still see the red and white poster that was taped to the back of our classroom wall. STOP, LOOK, AND LISTEN, it told us. What a lesson for a soulful life it gave us!

Stop. Take time. Midlife crisis (all of life's crises, really) and all of society encourage us to rush, to run helter-skelter here and there, to "make the most" out of the time we have. It all sounds wonderful until it crashes. We live our lives on a treadmill of urgency, when what we need to do instead is to take time. Take time to eat together instead of grabbing a fast meal. Take time to celebrate. Take time to look into the face of a loved one. Take time to experience and not to miss the beauty of the children in our lives as they grow up. Take time to do the things we love. Take time to think about what we want from life. Take time to grieve. Take time to appreciate the people, places, and things that are around us now. Take time to see God's hand in the crazy quilt of our experiences.

Look. Someone once said, "All things are possible for the one who knows how to see." Soulful living means learning to see that there is more to ourselves and our lives than the things that limit us and trouble us, more even than those that have limited us all through our lives. A friend who is a recovering alcoholic, now a famous author and sober for many years, tells me that the real issue behind his alcoholism was the issue of freedom: Would he allow himself to be free from the limitations of his addiction? "I had to look beyond my personal history, the abusiveness of my childhood, the ridicule and failure and poverty that were a part of my everyday existence, and to see that I was being called out of all of that and into freedom." For many years, he closed the door by abusing substances. Then one day something inside him made him see the possibility of transcending his limitations. He said yes, and has not taken a drink since.

As a writer, I am profoundly aware of the tyranny of a blank piece of paper. There are days when a blank screen on my computer or a blank sheet in the typewriter will hold my mind and imagination hostage for hours. To get past that, I have to look beyond the limits of the page, remind myself that my mind and my soul are bigger and more powerful than the mental blank I am experiencing, and just get down to writing. Once I have written a few words, things usually begin to flow. I may edit those words and sentences heavily later on, but the point is to get beyond the block and into the flow. When we are soulful, we learn to look beyond our limitations, to look and see who we really are and what we can really accomplish.

Listen. Once we stop and allow ourselves to look at who we really are, we need to listen. Always listen, and listen carefully. The notion of transcending our limitations can take us straight in the direction of the ego, which puffs us up and makes us think we are a law unto ourselves. I understand that there is a type of mental disorder called bipolarity (sometimes known as manic-depression), in the more severe forms of which people might come to imagine that they can fly like a bird. We don't need to have that illness in order to know what those delusions are like; our egos are constantly telling us how important we are or how important we wish everyone else would make us out to be. As we learn to live soulfully, however, we come to the realization that since we are made in the image and likeness of God, we have no need for any further importance. We are already as important as we need to be. When we are doing what we are supposed to be doing, when we are following the course that God sets for us in guiding us to soulfulness, we do not need to be any more important than we are. A friend of mine who is an announcer with a long career in radio once told me about the time he was fired from a large radio station and went to work for a small station. "I discovered," he told me, "that if I couldn't be as professional on a small station as I was on a large station, I shouldn't be in the business." By the same token, when we listen to the voice of God calling us, we know that, wherever we are, we are important enough. Today, I sit at a desk on the nineteenth floor of a twenty-story office building, talking to radio audiences, writing, speaking to the public. Perhaps someday I shall be confined to a sickbed, able to contact very few. Am I more important now than I will be then? Will I be less important then than I am now? How I answer depends entirely on whether I am listening to the voice of God rather than to the voice of ego. The voice of God will be in both situations, guiding me, helping me to fulfill a purpose. If I listen now, chances are that I will listen then. If I listen to the voice that tells me my life is more important now than it will be then, it is the voice of ego that I am hearing. Listening to the divinity within me tells me that today and tomorrow are of equal importance, that my importance comes from being present to the One who made me and who loves me and who will always find something for me to do and to be in His world.

Stop. Look. Listen. They are the keys to soul. Midlife crises may come and go. Everything we think we cherish and cannot do without may come and go. We can complain. We can rant and rave. We can deny. We can blame. Or we can allow ourselves to stop, look, and listen, and to discover beneath it all the presence of God.

Chapter Eleven

The Language of Soul

*T*he computer screen told me that the caller had said she was an agnostic, and that she hoped it was all right to call. When I took the call, she told me she was open to the possibility of God, to the presence of God, but she just couldn't bring herself to say for sure that God existed. She was in real turmoil about this, and wondered if I could help.

As we talked on the air, I noticed that this woman had a beautiful laugh, one that came right from the heart. She told me about her cats, whom she cared for and loved very much. It struck me that there was a great deal of love in this woman's life. I felt that her laughter and her loves were great touchstones in her search for God. It also occurred to me that her experience of God had been a vacuum. She wanted to find God, but found only empty space. As we talked, I wondered whether the best thing for her might be to hold on to both sides of her experience at the same time. If she could focus on the beauty and love in her life and at the same time realize that there was a void where God should be, she might have a chance of eventually finding God. I was struck at how touched she was when I mentioned the beauty of her laugh and the wonder of her love for her cats. I told her that if she continued to focus on the absence of God exclusively, that is what she would get. If, on the other hand, she could be open to seeing the beauty in her life as somehow divine, she might be able to watch the void slowly being filled.

It seems to me that the position of this woman, who called herself an agnostic, was not that much different from those of us who call ourselves believers. Most of us focus on the absence of God a great deal of the time. Our lives become filled with the stuff of our calendars, with gossip, the TV talk shows, the highlights of the evening news. Though believers, we lose our sense of God.

Christianity has a doctrine that is similar in tone to the Buddhist teaching "When the student is ready, the teacher will appear." Christianity's doctrine of divine providence is similar in that it carries the notion that the events of our lives can be guides for us on our journey. But it is different because it tells us that it is God whom we encounter at the bottom of our coincidences, and that with his help, we can alter the course of the events in our experiences. God's work of redemption includes taking the evil and chaos and disorder in the world and bringing love and depth and goodness out of them.

To most of us, that sounds like a tall tale indeed. Most of us have felt the impact of personal tragedies. We look at the world and all that goes on. "Where is God?" we say. Like the Psalmist, we sigh and implore, "Out of the depths I cry to you, O Lord. Lord, hear my voice." We wonder, if God truly exists, why he does not do something about the terrible tragedies that are the daily lot of human beings.

The soul tells another story. In the face of temporal confusion, the soul speaks the language of eternity.

The Hindus have a way of describing how the soul speaks the language of eternity; they call it "the Observer." Way down beneath our experiences, even beneath our knowing, there is the one who observes the suffering and the knowing going on within us. Robert Frost said it in his poem "The Secret": "We all sit around in a ring and suppose./But the Secret sits in the middle and knows."

When I first encountered the Observer, I was frightened to death. I thought there was something very much the matter with me. I was in the second grade in school, and we were coming inside from recess. Climbing the stairs to get back to the room, I suddenly had a profound experience of my own uniqueness. It occurred to me that I could see the faces of other people, but I could not see my own face. Everybody else was Peter or Bill or Mary, but I was, well, "I." It was frightening to me not to be like everybody else. The experience subsided, but the meaning never really left me. Why was I not like the others?

It was years before I became aware of what my experience meant. That experience of "I," of my own uniqueness, was an experience of "the Observer," the mystery of my being, who sits in the middle of my life and knows, profoundly knows, what is taking place.

When it dawned on me who or what this was, I realized that this was the One who had been there all along, who was the center of my existence, the depth of my soul. As a college student, as a seminarian, when I felt my heart burn within me as I sat in prayer in front of the Blessed Sacrament in a Catholic church or chapel, that Observer was the one who was present, burning within me, comforting me, guiding me. When I lay near death in the hospital, mysteriously knowing that I was not going to die despite what everyone else was saying, it was the Observer, God within me, who lay there beneath my anxiety and physical weakness and let me know that everything was going to be all right.

What is this thing we are calling the Observer? The Hindus think that it is one of the manifestations of God, and I think they are right.

As we become soulful, our lives become infused with a genuine intimacy with God. We become aware of a presence deep within us that is not the same as our egos, or our feelings, or even ourselves. While all of those are present, we are aware of a dimension within us that is none of these. In that space, in that dimension, something deep, something remarkable, is going on. My caller who defined herself as an agnostic on one level had, on another level, learned to speak the language of love. I knew this from her laughter and from her love of animals. Discovering that dimension deep within us is like discovering a whole new dimension to our lives. It is a dimension we can learn to draw on to enhance our living. If we take time to focus on that deeper dimension, to cultivate it, we can learn to hear its language and to speak it. We can learn to understand its message for us, and to know that its message leads us to new and wonderful levels of living, levels that we were made to enjoy.

Until we allow ourselves to become aware of the deeper dimensions of soul, we do not realize what we are missing. Coleman Barks in *The Essential Rumi* tells the story about a cow who walked across the entire city of Baghdad, ignoring all the sights and wonders of the city and seeing only some hay that had fallen off a wagon. Until we experience that deeper dimension within ourselves, we are like that cow. We can travel all over the world, yet miss the true beauty and depth of it. I am reminded of a fellow professor years ago, a man who all his life had longed to go to Europe and finally was able to spend an entire summer in England and France. When I greeted him upon his return, I asked excitedly, "How was Europe?" His answer was, "Fine." No travel brochure writer, he.

Too many of us spend our lives looking at the world and at our own lives in a one- or two-dimensional way. We see suffering, we may even develop some insight into it, but we miss the magic and the joy of living. "The best you can do," we say, "is maybe to get a little wisdom so you don't make the same mistakes all over again." I remember in high school and college hearing that the reason for taking history courses was to learn the mistakes of the past so as not to repeat them. It would have been better, I think, to have said that we study history in order to learn from the successes of the past so as to repeat them. That is certainly a much more positive view, and, I believe, a lot more fun. But even that does not compare with the joy of simply falling in love with history. Watch a history buff sometime, someone who can make the fall of Rome or the Middle Ages come alive. Their rapture is contagious. That is what it is like when we fall in love with life, when we discover an intimacy with God, the secret who sits in the middle, knowing and loving us.

How is that possible? Our suspicion is that finding your soul happens to only a few. Spiritually, many of us feel the way we feel about winning the lottery: The winner is always somebody else, never ourselves. But really, the joy of finding our soul is available to everyone; all of us can learn to listen to the language of soul, and to speak it.

How do you find your soul? Partially by invitation, and partially by choice.

You find your soul by invitation. In the *Bhagavad Gita*, Arjuna is called by Krishna to a life of "acting without experiencing the fruits of action." The Buddha is called to enlightenment under the Bodhi tree. The prophets are called by a direct act of God. The heart of Mohammed is opened by angels and filled with light. Mary is called by an angel to be the Mother of God. Jesus is called at his baptism in the River Jordan and again at his transfiguration on the mountain. One does not enter the world of soul by one's own efforts or on one's own merits. One is called to hear and to speak the language of soul.

When is the call given? The calls that lie at the heart of the great religions were given in intense personal moments. Most of us, however, do not experience anything like a voice from God or an apparition. Nonetheless, we can receive calls to soulful living. They can come in various ways, and almost always catch one unawares. A woman told me that on a visit to the Cloisters, she found the medieval museum so enchanting that she was inspired to create a meditative garden in the backyard of her home. This, for her, marked the revival of a long-dormant interest in beautifying her home and living in soulful surroundings. Countless times I have had telephone calls during radio programs from people who have told me, "You know, I am listening to you for the first time. I just happened to tune in the radio and there you were." Each time, they then proceeded to tell me about an important personal problem, something that has kept them from living with soul.

Soulful living is a call. Sometimes it is the realization of a series of calls. For me personally, I have come to the awareness that my invitations to soulfulness have been coming for a long time. My parents' deaths, my illness, the joy of helping others in church and in the media, the pleasure of music, art, and nature—all of these have been part of an ongoing call to find my soul. So when, during a vacation some months back, I decided that it was time for me to take my soul seriously, I knew that my readiness to do that was both an invitation in itself and the result of thousands of other invitations—Wordsworth called them "intimations of immortality"—that I had been receiving most of my life.

There is an invitation to soulfulness, but soulfulness also involves a decision. The beauty and depth of soulful living come only after we have decided that we will not live any other way. We begin to take seriously the question of Jesus, "What does it profit someone to gain the whole world and suffer the loss of their soul? Or what would a person give in exchange for their soul?" As Thomas Moore has so pointedly told us in one of his best-selling books, we must learn to care for our souls.

Caring for our souls involves a kind of discipline, which has a special meaning for me as a priest. Years ago, a priest assigned to assist the pastor of a parish was known as a curate. *There* is a word with soul. The title "curate" comes from the Latin word *cura*, which means "care." It implies that the parish priest is the one who has the care of souls, the *cura animarum.* The French call their parish priest *curé,* a word that carries the same connotation. Jean Vianney, the sainted priest from Ars who heard confessions by the hour, is known to Catholics as the Curé of Ars.

The work of a priest (or other clergyperson) is considered to be that of caring for souls. This work takes on many dimensions, the best known of which is the conducting of services. But beyond this, the clergyperson is the one who is considered to be primarily responsible for the spiritual welfare of the people. Whatever their faith, clergy are charged with the task of caring for the souls of the faithful. In their houses of worship, in their parlors, in the homes and hospitals they visit, theirs is the task of enhancing the soulfulness of the members of their respective flocks.

But responsibility for care of the soul is not exclusively that of the clergy. It is the charge of all of us. The title "curate" serves as a reminder of the task that awaits us all. No matter what way or state or time of life be ours, we are called to elicit soulfulness from within ourselves and from the world. Made in the image and likeness of God, whose nature is to bring good out of evil, we are charged with the task of taking what is often an evil and unfriendly world and endowing it with a friendliness, a homeyness, a soul.

Insofar as soulfulness is both an invitation and a choice, it is not meant to be something fleeting. Rather, it is meant to be a permanent home in which we live. Traditionally, a new husband carries his bride across the threshold of their new home to begin their life together. Crossing the threshold symbolizes "no turning back." Similarly, soulful living is intended to be crossing a threshold. In each of our lives, there comes a point where we are no longer willing to live any other way but soulfully. What Gerard Manley Hopkins describes as the "dearest freshness deep down" becomes so dear, so precious, that we do not want to live without it.

The magic of soulfulness lies first of all in an initial call to it. Then there comes the decision to appreciate that moment as it happens. Finally, there is the decision to take the moment within so that it can be re-created. You cross a threshold: You decide that you are not going to live without the magic of soulfulness again. You consent to make the language of soul your mother tongue.

The magic of soulfulness takes its life from the principle that we are what we pay attention to. What we pay attention to grows and multiplies. When we allow ourselves to be enchanted by the magic of soul, we find more and more instances of soulfulness showing up in our lives.

When Jesus said "The kingdom of God is

within you," he was talking about finding your soul. Finding your soul, in the fullest sense, means finding and cultivating a sense of God, and deciding that never again do you want to live without that.

Creating the conditions for soulfulness is like learning a foreign language: You have to immerse yourself in it in order to master it. Most of us remember a few phrases at best of the language we learned in high school or college. Unless we immerse ourselves in a language, speaking and listening to it every day, the language will never be ours. Similarly, finding our souls means putting ourselves on a daily basis in the presence of soulfulness. Just as a squirrel stores up nuts for the winter, so must we store up images and embodiments of soul.

In his book *Real Magic,* Wayne Dyer suggests that each of us create a "real magic" zone in our mind. We may at times feel very skeptical about our ability to experience magic in life, but Dyer says that we should dedicate one special part of our inner life as a shrine to it.

We might be more inclined to live in the magic of soul and to hear its language if we were to restore for ourselves the concept of the sabbath. The original sabbath was the seventh day, on which God rested from the labors of creation. In our society, there is no longer a real sabbath, as there used to be. In most places, stores are open, people work on the sabbath, our Saturdays and Sundays are just like every other day. In order to keep alive a sense of soulfulness, we must carve out some significant block of time when we do not work, but rest and devote ourselves to true leisure and to the pursuit of beauty in nature, in the arts, in our loved ones. That sabbath time enables us to keep ourselves in touch with soulfulness each and every day and to stay attuned to the language of soul.

Living soulfully is a decision, the crossing of a threshold. When we make the decision to find our souls and when we sustain that decision through prayer and immersion in the beautiful and the gracious, we will find, I truly believe, that our world has become a very blessed place indeed. The Bible tells us that the world was created through the Word of God, and that the Word became flesh and dwelt amongst us. As we learn to speak and hear the Word of God in the depths of our souls and in the beauty of his world, we find ourselves at home in a new dimension of living—we become fluent in the language of soul.

Chapter Twelve

Soulful Choices

*T*he soul does not go for quick fixes, avoidance, the speed of the present age. The soul takes the long view of life, a view that can sometimes drive modern society crazy.

Today, the office next to mine is experiencing a computer problem: Something in the board refuses to allow printing on the parallel port. There is a repairman in the office now attempting to fix it, and he will. We are accustomed to that in our society, and we make the mistake of thinking that our relationships, our personal lives, our families, and so forth can be fixed if only we can find the right repairman. So we tinker. We tinker with immigration reform, welfare reform, reform of medical insurance, ways to alternately legalize and prevent prayer in school, and we wonder why, after all that, our society never seems to be better off and less divided.

The problem with all of this is that we never ask the right questions. Years ago, Frank Sheed wrote in his book *Society and Sanity* that the essential requirement for sanity is that one know what it means to be a human being. When society loses its ability to define human nature, it loses its sanity, its sense of direction.

Just as we as individuals have souls, so our society has a soul. Finding your soul has not only an individual aspect, it also has a societal aspect. In trying to address the good of the world, it is not enough that we look to what is good for our individual souls as though they were discrete and unconnected with the soul of the world. We need also to look to making the world a better place. That was, in part, the thrust of what Krishna was saying to Arjuna in the *Bhagavad Gita*, telling him that he must go to war. It was the thrust of Ulysses' realization that, though he was reluctant to go into battle, he must, for the good of his country. Our nations, our world, have souls, and it is our responsibility to make whatever contribution we can to finding and caring for those souls as well as for our own.

It seems to be a revelation to men and women today that their nation or their world has a soul. When addressing groups of married people, I tell them that their marriage has a soul. Frequently, that is a surprise to them. The husband knows that he has a soul; the wife knows that she has a soul. Often that means little enough to them, and it takes some time to get them to think in terms of a soul in their marriage. I tell them that it is the soul of their marriage that should be the chief focus of their concern. If they argue constantly, and never sit down to dinner together, and are inconsiderate to each other, cheat on each other, and try to find as many excuses as possible to be away from each other, each of those problems can be fixed. But they could fix them all and still not have a soulful marriage. Conversely, a very soulful marriage can incorporate disagreements and absences and misunderstandings, alongside romance and communication and forgiveness. The soulfulness is what makes it worthwhile. It is what fuels everything else.

In the same way, our nation has a soul and our world has a soul. There is a tonality, a purpose, to them. It is difficult for us to keep a sense of this as we read the daily news accounts of the events that take place there, but we must recover a sense of soul for our nation and our world. Having lost a sense of their soulfulness, we have lost a sense of their direction. We have lots of ideas and suggestions and policies. But without soul, these are pointless.

We have lost our moral compass, I believe, because we have tried to declare things to be true north that really are not. I have been thinking a great deal lately about the choices we make and how we make them. Increasingly, I am coming to believe that our inability to find our souls, personally and in society, has a great deal to do with our misguided understanding of choice.

For much of our society, "choice" has become true north, the be-all and end-all of human existence. We talk about being "pro-life" or "pro-choice" when it comes to abortion, and we talk about the so-called right to choose death in the face of suffering. We become incensed when we detect that someone is taking away from us our ability to choose.

The difficulty with this emphasis on choice is that it ignores the fact that choice does not belong on center stage all by itself. In order to function as it is meant to in our lives, choice needs a partner. There is always something that we choose, and some things that we choose are right and others are wrong, even though people disagree on what makes them so.

For a truly soulful approach to our personal and societal lives, we cannot stop at the notion of choice. Important though choice is, it cannot stand alone as the fundamental touchstone of our existence or of our decisions.

Another popular candidate for the true north of our lives is the concept of values. We hear so much about them these days; indeed, it is difficult to go through a day without hearing at least once the challenge to bring our society back to proper values. It seems to me that our current focus on values misses the true depth of our lives. It doesn't say anything, really; it only sounds as if it said something. Think about it. Anything can be a value—all that is required is someone to value it, and if you wait long enough, you will find someone to value almost anything. The problem is, some values are right values and others are wrong values, and we need a basis for distinguishing one from the other.

What if we went deeper in our consideration of the true touchstone of our moral decisions that either choice itself or values themselves? What if, instead, we looked to our true depth, the depths of our souls, and began to reflect that within our souls lie powers—generally called virtues—that direct us to the good for which we are intended? Prudence, justice, courage, moderation, faith, hope, love—these guides or powers are the true guides that come from the very depths of our souls that enable us to make soulful choices in our relationships, which enable us to choose values that are sound rather than values that are not.

Let's take an example. When a married couple comes to me full of animus and hostility, there is, of course, the possibility that they are at the end of their marriage. Often enough, in the present tenor of our society, divorce is the option they are led to consider. Despite that, I refuse to assume automatically that their marriage is necessarily over. Frequently their conflicts are over values: He feels she should spend more time at home, for example, while she feels she has the right to more independence. Once the values have been aired, once the conflicts have had their voice, then I start looking deeper. Do they have the courage to stand by their commitment? Do they fundamentally love each other and their children? Do they have faith and hope so that, despite their hurts and their rocky past, their marriage can come to be a blessing to themselves and to the world? Are they open to the possibility that underneath the storms and conflicts over values there is a mystery that can be described only as the mystery of love? What I am looking for, notice, are not just choices or values. I am looking for prudence, justice, fortitude, temperance, faith, hope, love—powers within them (and within their marriage) that lead them to be the best they can be. I am looking to see whether they can hear a challenge from the depths of their souls, and whether they can grow to accept that challenge once they have heard it.

An eye-opener for me in recent years has been the realization that the deeper life of a marriage may be experienced by only one of the two spouses. The other spouse may already be out the door, but the remaining wife or husband continues to believe, to pray, to work at better ways of relating. Before long, the spouse who gave up begins to see a difference in the other partner, and a basis for reconciliation is formed. I am indebted to Susan Zappo, who graciously shared this notion with me, gleaned from her pioneer work in marriage restoration, and who has seen many marriages repaired when originally only one partner was committed to it. It has helped me not to be superficial about my own work with couples, especially when they tell me that they believe their marriage is over.

In making soulful choices, we need to realize that conflict over values is part of life. It strains our relationships, yes, but it need not end them. In a friendship, in a marriage, in a society, the questions are, Do we believe that our relationship is deeper than our present conflicts, deeper than our past mistakes and hurts and even infidelities? Is there something down deep that we are willing to work to preserve?

That something deeper to believe in, I would submit, is the soul of the marriage, the friendship, the society. The early years of a marriage—bearing and raising children, getting to know each other, absorbing financial strain—can total it unless there is that something deeper to believe in. We can do values clarification forever. We can read books, take courses, go to counseling, all can be helpful. But there must also be a commitment to soul, to the "something more" around us, beyond us, framing who we are.

This is true of priests as well. The soul of my priesthood, twenty-one years after ordination, has seen some rocky ground. I have lived in good situations, bad situations, experienced success, failure, betrayal, companionship, support, and joy. I have been a good priest to some people and I have not been so good to others. I am a priest today not just because I choose to be, nor simply because I value being a priest. Those are factors, but they are not the soul of my priesthood.

I am a priest because from the depths of my being, I find myself called to priesthood, called to capacities for believing, hoping, loving, caring, and courage that are not just things I value, but powers and gifts and calls that I discover from within. What I experience in those things I am calling virtues—powers of soul—is the abiding, loving, caring presence of God.

There are no formulas by which to measure soulful choosing, because ultimately it is guided by mystery. Why does a wife suddenly fall in love with her husband all over again in the canned-goods aisle of the supermarket? Why do I fall in love with my priesthood when I am sitting at the bedside of a dying friend?

But that is just the point. Try as we might to make choice the arbiter of our lives, try as we might to ascribe rightness of life to values, fundamentally it is neither of these that makes our lives and our choices soulful. It is the immeasurable, intangible, enabling, deepening, life-giving capacity to say yes to why we are here, even in the face of ridiculous circumstances, unlikely people, and incomprehensible moments.

I thought about this the other day when, in the midst of a busy day at the office, the phone rang and it was my friend Jean calling. I have known Jean for many years now, and she is a wonderful businesswoman, wife, and mother, a woman of profound faith. She has struggled with a business and I have struggled with a radio ministry, and over the years we have listened to each other's ups and downs, consoled each other, and celebrated each other's successes. When I think about coincidences, I think of how she and I came to meet. It was the beginning of another week of trying to get enough sponsors to pay for that week's radio program. (That's how I did it in those early days.) I saw an ad in one of the Catholic newspapers, made a cold call, and Jean answered the phone. As we talked, a friendship was born. Each of us sensed that the other was not simply running a business, but performing a ministry that, we hoped, would make the world a little better and bring people closer to God. Right away there was a kind of "aha" experience in which each of us understood the other's mission very deeply. For many years now, we have been friends, mostly by phone, for there have not been many occasions when we have actually seen each other.

Today, when Jean called, I knew there was something different; I could hear it in her voice.

"Father," she said, "I have cancer. I am going to have surgery."

I tried to sound calm, but I could feel a lump forming in my throat. We talked for several minutes, and what amazed me was how real, how honest, Jean was able to be about all of her feelings. Everything was there: her fear, her anxiety, her gratitude for the support of her family, but most of all, her faith. There was no doubt about it, Jean truly believed that the Lord was at her side, and would be there throughout her ordeal.

It was a soulful conversation, and we were able to express our gratitude for the long friendship we had shared. With all my heart, I wanted to do something, to say a word or perform a deed that would be caring, consoling, that would make the searing nature of this experience go away for Jean.

"What can I do?" I asked, hoping she would give me a task or an assignment.

"Father," she replied, "what you can do is pray for me. That's what I need you to do."

Of course I'll pray for you, I thought, but can't I *do* something? I felt frustrated, helpless.

And then I understood. Jean was not putting me off, not politely sweeping aside my request to help. She was asking me to do the very thing I am called to do as a priest: to pray for people. A priest may comfort, console, forgive, listen, officiate, but above all else, he prays for people. My ego wanted to do something more tangible, more "important," but in her goodness, Jean called me back to the very thing I was ordained to do: to pray for her, to be a conduit between herself and the mystery of God. It is not that I pray more capably or more successfully than anyone else; it is rather that as a priest, I am called to be the official connection between the souls of the suffering and the soul of God.

It is the same for the mother or father who sits all hours of the night at the bedside of a sick child. With all their hearts, they want to do something to take the pain and illness away. But their greatest calling, their real calling, is to be there, just to be there, and in being there to let their souls enfold their dear one's soul in the warmth of their love and the love of God.

In a marriage, in parenting, in ministry, in business, in soulful living of any kind, soulful choosing means creating an atmosphere in which someone's heart and soul can touch the heart and soul of God.

When we do this, we get in touch with God within. As we accustom ourselves to living with soul and making soulful decisions, we refuse to accept the elixirs for peace and the superficial approaches to social problems that are foisted upon us on a daily basis. Just as we have souls, our nation has a soul, our world has a soul and a mission. As we come to make better, more soulful, moral decisions that focus on what is deepest and dearest within us, we will begin to think twice about what is really good for society. We will find ourselves called to make our moral decisions against the background of the purpose for which we are alive. We will discover that soulful living has a transformative power that enables us to return to the everydayness of life, and to find there the sacred mystery of God.

Chapter Thirteen

You *Do* Have
a Prayer

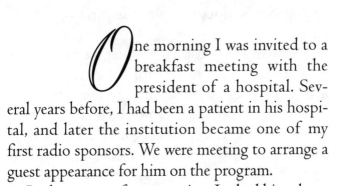

*O*ne morning I was invited to a breakfast meeting with the president of a hospital. Several years before, I had been a patient in his hospital, and later the institution became one of my first radio sponsors. We were meeting to arrange a guest appearance for him on the program.

In the course of our meeting, I asked him about the various facets of his job. "Being a hospital president," he told me, "is like being the mayor of a small city. I have to think about security, sanitation, food and clothing, hiring and paying workers, and on and on. And all of that along with the practice of medicine." Seeing it that way enabled me to understand the complexity of his job. Clearly, he reveled in the complexity, which was in itself an astounding fact.

Many of us, however, find complexity difficult. "Give me the simple life," the song says, and most of us would love to have that as our theme. Our reality is the exact opposite of that. We feel pressured on so many fronts. We have domestic worries, financial worries, problems on the job. Getting to and from work is a hassle for many people. Even our leisure time is pressured, as we try to stay on top of errands, Little League games, the laundry. If we do get a moment to relax, we often end up simply flopping mindlessly in front of the television.

My friend the hospital president is not all that different from the rest of us: We are all like the mayors of small cities. We have so much to do, so little time to do it in, so much to think about. Most of us are really prisoners of schedules and responsibilities. Not everyone finds in the complexity of his or her life the joy and positive challenge that my friend found in his complex job at the hospital. For many, complexity is a problem, not a source of joy.

Time management programs can give us some

help, and there are some programs that encourage us to look at our life goals and values when deciding how to use our time. But we need more than time management if we are going to live with the peacefulness we desire and for which we were made. We certainly need more than new methods of leisure, new toys. What we need, I think, is the daily practice of prayer. Prayer is what keeps us close to God, to the divine within us, to the very depths of our soul. Prayer keeps us in touch with our mission on earth, and enables us to keep our sense of mission alive when we are down or overwhelmed. Without prayer, we don't have a prayer of managing our lives.

The mere mention of prayer makes some people nervous. They think prayer is for priests, ministers, or saints, and they are afraid that they don't qualify. They think that prayer is complicated and involves a lot of words or memorization. Others feel that prayer takes too much time, and their schedules are already too busy. Still others will admit that they simply don't know how to pray, that prayer requires too much skill and theological know-how.

The fact is, prayer is none of those things. Certainly, the saints prayed, but they also taught other people how to pray. No genuine saint ever claimed that his or her prayer was his or her exclusive property. True saints are delighted to share their intimacy with God. Prayer is for everyone.

Prayer is not complicated. For those who do not know what to say, there is a wide variety of prayer books and traditional prayers readily available. But when people tell me they do not know how to pray, I often tell them just to use their own words. If they are feeling angry or hopeless or joyous, they can simply tell God what is in their heart. "Out of the depths I cry to you, O Lord," the Psalmist said, and we, too, can pray out of the depths of our hearts and souls. Prayer can be wordless as well. One can simply sit in awe before the beauty of a sunset, sit quietly in a house of worship or in one's own house. I have known men and women whose prayer, in a moment of grief, was their weeping. I have known people who, in a moment of joy, prayed through dance. I know people who keep a small Bible or prayer book by their side at work, and I know others who bow their heads when they pass a house of worship. One does not need to be a genius to pray, and you don't have to use complicated techniques. Prayer is as simple as it can be.

Prayer does not necessarily take a lot of time. Many of us do find it helpful to sit quietly in prayer for an extended period in the morning and/or at night. Frankly, I do think that most of us need one extended period of prayer at least weekly in order to center ourselves in God. But the length of the prayer does not matter as much as finding an effective way to experience the presence of God in our lives.

Personally, I need to begin my day quietly. I have been amazed at what a difference this has made in my life. I am calmer as I go through the day. When I do not make time for quiet prayer at the start of my day, the day goes less smoothly. My periods of prayer and meditation are such that they place me and my day directly in the hands of God.

I can already hear people saying, "Well, that's fine for you. You don't have to rush to get a family ready, and make a six A.M. train or bus or drive through rush-hour traffic to get to work." Of course they are right. In that respect, I have a much simpler life than many people. However, my experience in parish work tells me that there are many busy, professional people, many of them parents, who take time at the start of their day to come to church. This tells me that it's possible not just for people like me, but for family people and commuters as well, to carve out some quiet time before work. My other thought in response to the objection is that, before I made the effort to create that quiet time, I could have given you a host of reasons why I could never do it. I was too tired, I had to get ready for work, get the laundry together, feed the cats, and so on. Now, my mind is quiet, and I find that I can do all of those things and still have my prayerful time to read, meditate, and eat. The quietness of my mind, heart, and soul makes everything go better.

Some people simply cannot pray in the morning, for a host of reasons, but do find they prefer quiet time in midday or at night. Prayer is something one can do at any time; the trick, of course, is actually to make it a part of one's routine. Sometimes, because we know that we can pray at any time, we put it off to some indefinite time in the future. Making a definite time for prayer lets our souls know that we are serious about wanting peace, beauty, and ongoing encounter with God in our lives. Our souls are very subtle, and if we give them the impression that everything else in our lives is more important than prayer, or can take precedence over our prayer, then they will not believe we are serious about having peace or a sense of God. The importance of regular prayer is something of which many of the world religions are very well aware. For example, the Catholic Church requires its priests and religious to pray at regular times in the morning, in the afternoon, in the evening, and at night. This prayer, called the Liturgy of the Hours, provides a rhythm of prayer and reflection in one's day. Ignatius of Loyola, in founding the Jesuits, instructed them to make an examination of conscience at midday and in the evening. In both cases, the idea is to carry the sense of God throughout one's daily life.

If we want to have a greater sense of simplicity in our lives, this will not necessarily be accomplished by time management. We must first turn within, find a place, a sense of peace in our souls, and create the time in our day to nurture that. At least half the battle lies in convincing our souls that we really want the peace and harmony in our lives that we say we want. Our souls will be convinced only when we take steps to anchor quiet meditative time into our day.

Prayer is a deeply personal matter; there is no one universally correct way to pray. I think the only rule of thumb is that one's posture should not be sloppy or indifferent. One can pray kneeling down, lying down, sitting down, standing up, bowing, in the lotus position, or in any combination of those positions. What matters is that one find a position or posture that helps one to experience a deep inner peace. If you find yourself getting restless, change positions.

What do you do during your quiet time? There is a variety of ways of praying. When I was beginning to meditate, I found it helpful to read carefully a passage from Scripture and think about what I could learn from it, and direct some conversation about it back to God. Later, I preferred to walk up and down while reading a passage very slowly, getting a feel for the beauty of the words, letting them touch my soul. Sometimes I sit quietly in a church or chapel and let the sense of God's presence wash over me and through me. Sometimes I will sit and talk over a problem with God, and listen for whatever guidance comes from the depths of my soul.

One of the forms of prayer I have found especially helpful has been the prayer of affirmation. In really troubled times, I have found that it is not enough merely to focus on my problems and worries and negative thoughts in prayer. At times, I have found myself feeling more worried and more agitated, especially since I do not tend to hear physically the voice of God responding to my pleas. As a result, I can begin to wonder whether my prayer is having any effect, and that can be very discouraging. If I am not careful, my prayer can become a mere rehashing of all the negative things I am concerned about. At times like this I find that my soul needs some new ideas, some better ideas, to focus on. That is where affirmations help me. They do not deny the reality of my worries, but they provide something stronger and more powerful than the worries to think about.

Affirmations can work because of the way our souls work. Our soul is like a magnet, drawing into itself whatever it focuses on. For example, if I believe that my life is a walking disaster, I will draw into my life the people and the situations that will create more and more disaster. This happens to people all the time; we almost take it for granted. The student who says "I'm no good in math" wonders why he fails his math tests. The colleague who says "Every winter I get at least three colds" wonders why he is coughing and sneezing. The friend who laments "I can't balance my checkbook" wonders why he is always overdrawn. Our statements and beliefs tend to be self-fulfilling prophecies. If, in a crisis, we say "I'm ruined," we probably are. Subconsciously, like magnets, we draw into our lives the people, places, and situations that will reinforce what we believe. It is amazing.

Affirmations give us something else to think about. They give us options, free us up from the limits that our situations appear to impose upon us. They make our souls sit up and take notice, and at least consider drawing something different to themselves.

By affirmations I mean positive statements that reflect beliefs we have or manifestations that we desire. Here are a few that I use from time to time.

God is the source of all my supply, and his voice is the only one I hear.

Everything I need comes to me easily and effortlessly.

I surrender my soul into the hands of God and I receive everything I need.

I am guided by the Light of God within me.

This or something better is now manifesting for me.

The Bible is replete with powerful affirmations:

The Lord is my Shepherd; there is nothing I shall want.

The Lord is my life's refuge; of whom should I be afraid?

I can do all things in Christ who strengthens me.

The kinds of affirmations we choose for prayer are important to notice. Our affirmations must not threaten any other belief of ours. Our souls may be easily influenced, but they are not stupid. People sometimes try courses of affirmations that outright deny their present experience. I have known of people in dire straits who have gone about affirming "I am as rich as Rockefeller" and have wondered why their situation hasn't improved. The reason is that when confronted with a statement that is so blatantly out of touch with their experience, the soul simply says, "Give me a break. What do you take me for, a fool?" What is needed is the kind of affirmation that will enable the soul to be intrigued and that does not fly in the face of its present experience. Such an affirmation might be "God is the source of all my supply." To this, our soul can say, "Well, that is interesting. Let's see what happens." After a few repetitions, one is likely to notice that he or she is less disturbed about money matters, more trusting and confident, perhaps even meeting people who can help with resources and fresh ideas. One has a sense of being guided and protected by God. The soul then has reason to be impressed, and gradually begins to focus on the new positive beliefs as assuredly as it previously focused on the negative ones.

I believe strongly that affirmations are not techniques for getting what we want. They are, rather, ways of deepening our lives and putting us in touch with the divine. I mention this because I have met people who use affirmations as ways to get rich or improve their health. This is fine, except it does not do a great deal to refresh the soul. Affirmations are primarily ways of establishing our connection with God, who is the source of every good and who knows how to care for us better than we know how to care for ourselves. When we make it our goal to be close to God, we find that we are guided to the people and things we need.

In using affirmations, it is important that we

believe God will work out the details. Someone who affirms, "I am attracting to myself the perfect woman who is five foot seven, weighs 110 pounds, and has blond hair and blue eyes" is overdoing it. The simple affirmation "God is sending into my life the perfect wife for me" is much more to the point, for it allows God to work out the details. How we attain the peace or prosperity we desire is up to God. Most of the time, we do not succeed when we attempt to dictate the means and tell God what to do.

Besides affirmations, another effective way to pray is to enter imaginatively into scenes from the Scriptures. Suppose, for example, you were really having a problem starting each new day. You hate to leave the comfort of the bed, put your feet on the floor, and face the challenge. As a Hindu, you might profitably read the *Bhagavad Gita* and listen to the dialogue between Arjuna and Krishna, putting yourself, let us say, in the place of Arjuna. Let Arjuna's words about the fearsomeness of going into battle be your own as you prepare to start the day. Realize that you are feeling what Arjuna was feeling, all the reluctance to do battle once again. Listen to Krishna's words about doing one's duty and acting without experiencing the fruits of action. Allow your soul to be comforted and nourished by this dialogue. It is always amazing to see how so many of our everyday problems are much more universal in scope than we had imagined.

A Christian, feeling a similar reluctance to undertake the work of the day, might reflect on the Gospel scene in which Jesus, the night before his death, begs his Father to let the cup of his suffering pass him by. "But not my will," Jesus said, "but thine be done." Placing himself beside Jesus in that scene, a Christian might feel that he is not alone in facing his difficult day, but is aided and guided by the Lord.

You might do a similar exercise with the story of your life. If you are a Buddhist, you might place yourself in the shoes of the young prince as he leaves his life of innocence and encounters a sick man, a poor man, and two men fighting, and as he sits under the Bodhi tree, he receives illumination and becomes the Buddha. You might reflect on your own years of innocence, either the innocence of the womb or the innocence of childhood (some do not have an innocent childhood), and of how you came to realize that innocence was not the real story of life. Perhaps the greater part of your years have been similar to the Buddha's encounter with the forces of evil in the world, and now you are ready to sit still for some enlightenment, for finding your soul. Reading the four noble truths and the eightfold path of Buddhism, you wonder where the forces of self-interest have entered your life to prevent illumination and to cause suffering. You ponder how turning yourself away from self-interest—emptying yourself—could lead you to a life of enlightened compassion.

One whose life has been steeped in hedonism might, in meditation, parallel his or her life with that of St. Augustine. Reading Augustine's account of his early stealing and mischief, later fascination with sex and pagan religion, and his having a child out of wedlock, one might develop a sense of how one's own personal transgression has clouded the horizons of one's lifetime. Reading the account of the young pagan Augustine in the garden as he hears the voice telling him to "take and read" the Scriptures, one might feel a stirring in one's own heart that illumines one's reading of the sacred texts, and may find himself exclaiming with the Bishop of Hippo, "Late have I loved thee, beauty so ancient and so new. Late have I loved thee."

Prayer can be reflective breathing, taking long slow breaths, repeatedly exhaling everything one does not want in one's life, and inhaling new air down to the very depths of one's soul. Modern Hinduism makes use of what is called a *siddhi* meditation in which, through rhythmic breathing, one shuts off one's mind and comes to the still point within one's soul from which one can instantly manifest the desires of one's heart.

Another way of praying is to take the traditional prayers of one's own faith and to pray them slowly, meditatively, word by word. Christians often recite the Lord's Prayer this way, pausing to reflect on the meaning of the words *Our*, *Father*, and so on. This is a very centering form of prayer, which takes them to their very depths and allows each word and the entire prayer to penetrate them to the core.

There are many ways of feeding and nourishing the soul, of giving it new ideas and freeing it from the limitations that daily life and humanity's common opinions impose.

We are, indeed, like mayors of small cities, but we can manage them with simplicity and grace. We have enormous responsibilities and are often weighed down by them, as we are by our pasts. The great secret is that we can be freed from the limitations this world imposes and that we can go to points deeper and broader than we often imagine.

Prayer is the way we do that. Whichever ways of prayer are ours, when we pray, we lift up our minds and hearts to God and bring ourselves to the still point from which all true simplicity comes. It is prayer that makes the small cities of our lives manageable, and that enables us to discover and to nurture the mystery of who we truly are.

Chapter Fourteen

The Gift to Be Simple

⌓

I don't know why I felt like singing this morning. I just did. Perhaps it was because, during my quiet time yesterday, I had been reading Richard Bode's *Beachcombing at Miramar* where he tells the story about his aunt, who in childhood encouraged him to sing. When he protested that he couldn't sing, she insisted that he should never say that and taught him how. I know the feeling. Until recently, until for whatever reason my voice has improved to the point of being able to carry a tune, I have been an awful singer. Ask anybody.

When I was in first grade, a Sister would come into our classroom every week to teach us singing. Eagerly, she divided us up into canaries, robins, bluebirds, and so on, and turned the bunch of us into a young chorus. Whenever I talk about that, people inevitably ask me, "And what kind of bird were you?" I tell them, "A pigeon." It isn't true, but it gets a laugh and glosses over the fact that singing is not my strong suit.

Pigeon or not—even a new, improved pigeon—I love music and love to sing. So I sing for myself and my cats, who at the very least pretend to be asleep when I do. I love the old Broadway musicals: *South Pacific, The King and I, Babes in Arms, The Sound of Music.* I love all kinds of music, but for singing, at least, these are my favorites.

But this morning, during my quiet time, my soul wanted none of these. Instead it chose the Shaker hymn "Simple Gifts." It is funny that it should have chosen that song. It is a particular favorite of everyone else's, but not of mine. I think it's mostly that I have heard it so many times. But that was the song my soul wanted this morning, and that was the song it bade me sing.

Within a few minutes, I realized why I had not fallen in love with "Simple Gifts." It was because I had never really paid attention to it, even though I had heard it so many times. This morning, it came alive for me. It was not just the words that worked the magic; it was the sheer act of making the words physical. Listening to music is heavenly. Listening to music in your head is great. But there is nothing like feeling the words as you hear them coming from your body. If you sing deep down from your diaphragm (where you are supposed to breathe when you sing), you can actually feel the vibration of the words as they come up from below, through your chest, and out your throat. My speech coach, Liz Dixon, used to talk about making an arc with the breath as it comes from the diaphragm and out the lips.

The power of "Simple Gifts" this morning was a really gentle, tender power. The music was like onomatopoeia: It produced the effect it signified. All of the Shaker gentleness and simple appreciation of life came forth from within me and flowed out into the words, making them dance, just as the notes dance in Copland's "Appalachian Spring."

The dancing gave a new lilt and so a new meaning to the words. Whereas before I had listened to the words and liked them but didn't fall in love, now the words danced before me, came to life, transformed my soul with their beauty and grace. It was as though I was hearing them for the first time.

'Tis the gift to be simple;
'Tis the gift to be free.
'Tis the gift to come down where we ought to be.
And when we find ourselves in the place just right,
'Twill be in the valley of love and delight.

When true simplicity is gained,
To bow and to bend we shan't be ashamed.
To turn, turn, will be our delight,
'Til by turning, turning, we come round right.

As I sang, I was simply stunned how the music created the simplicity it verbalized. It had the effect of a mantra, a secret chant, cleansing and purifying my soul like a whetstone. I felt simple and free. The lilt of the music caused my soul to lift, and when the music went down, my soul felt its depths.

It was then that I noticed the words. " 'Tis the gift to be simple": What an interesting expression! Not, as I used to think when I first heard the song years ago, *a* gift, but *the* gift.

How interesting that simplicity is described as a *gift*. Most of us think of simplicity as something we attain, not as something that is given to us. My experience in Mississippi showed me that simplicity was a gift. I was given a gift there, and an invitation to live my life in a different way. So many of us today are caught in the phenomenon of time management that we think that simplicity is some-thing we can create. The fact is, lasting simplicity begins inside us as an invitation, a gift.

It seems to me that, given simplicity, one can do almost anything. Simplicity is the clear vision of soul that makes one able to see possibilities.

This brings us to the next line of my morning song: "'Tis the gift to be free." How different from the popular song that says, "Freedom's just another word for nothin' left to lose." It seems to me that the Shakers have a much better idea of freedom, which is what is contained in the third line of the song: "'Tis the gift to come down where we ought to be." Freedom is the simplicity of vision that knows what our purpose is and en-ables us to come down to it.

As I sang those lines, I thought of myself sev-eral years ago, right after my mother got sick for the first time and I decided to put a hold on my graduate studies. It was a very confusing time, and I remember someone asking me what I would do if I could do anything at all with the rest of my life. I kind of looked about blankly and said, "I don't know." I was aware that I could do a number of things and do them well. I just didn't know what I wanted. How different it is for me now, knowing, as I do, that my purpose in life is to communicate inspiration and God's presence to people. Know-ing my purpose, where I ought to be, makes all the difference in the world. Before, I was certainly free to choose from a variety of options, which included things I could do well and things I had never tried. But I was not really free: I was imprisoned in my options. In fact, the number of options was absolutely frightening, almost paralyzing. Now, in the light of my overall purpose, I face options with a sense of excitement. I can't do them all, but I can consider them all.

That is what it means to be truly free. We are free when we are able to evaluate our options in the light of our overall purpose or mission. When we know our mission, we have "come down where we ought to be."

I sang my way into the second verse: "When true simplicity is gained/To bow and to bend we shan't be ashamed." Simplicity means being free, free within ourselves to choose whatever will assist us in fulfilling our purpose. When we are free, we are able to bow and to bend with situations and circumstances. When we are not free, we feel there is some shame or loss of face in flexibility.

As I reached the last lines of the song, the downward turn of the music at the end of the line indicated the depth on which the song ends. "To turn, turn will be our delight, 'til by turning, turning, we come round right."

I realized that the song was saying that simplicity, freedom, and flexibility were matters of purpose. Soulful freedom makes it possible for us to see life as an adventure, and to see the twists and turns of our lives as something to be enjoyed and appreciated for their beauty.

I thought back to the first evening of a retreat for married couples I was giving at the Passionist Spiritual Center in Riverdale, New York. Father Don Ware, the director of the center, took me for a walk along the grounds. He stopped in front of the main building and pointed to a large, flat patch of rock that decorated the landscape.

"You see how beautiful that rock is?" Father Don asked. I nodded. "Well, that rock existed ten thousand years ago. About then, a huge glacier was in this area, and it shifted the whole course of the river. Those crags and cracks you see in that rock are the product of that glacier."

Ten thousand years is a long time, but the effects of that glacier remained, and I could see them on other rock formations in the area as well. But what struck me so forcefully was not the vast expanse of time, but the rugged beauty of those rocks. I realized that those marks were the marks of damage done by the glacier. Yet those marks were a thing of beauty, mysteriously and skillfully woven into the being of the stone.

How often we try to hide our histories. We are ashamed of the wrong turns, the scars left by others. We try not to think about them. We see them as ugly. Yet from the perspective of our soul, from the perspective of God, those scars are part of the beauty of who we are. They can deepen us, give us wisdom, make us more caring and sensitive, more loving. Instead of being ashamed and covering up our scars, we must allow them to contribute to the purpose and beauty and flow of our lives.

Could it be, I wondered as I sang the last lines of "Simple Gifts," that we do not experience delight in the twists and turns in our lives because we are so concerned with appearances? Are we so afraid that if we ever admitted a mistake or floundered in life we would lose people's admiration? On the contrary, it seems we develop a soulful freedom in life only if we allow ourselves to delight in life's twists and turns. As I write this, I can hear my father's voice counseling me in his own wise way, years ago: "When you experience a storm in life, son, just sit tight and let the storm blow around you. Stay calm, and soon the storm will pass." My father had plenty of experience of that. There were times when, I know, he struggled to stay calm. He was a quiet man who loved peace and quiet, and who I think was always amazed at how stormy his life could be. My father never got up out of bed in the morning or went to bed at night without getting down on his knees and giving his day and his cares over to God. I don't think my father ever understood why, when he prayed for guidance and made a major move of job and family, he ended up in a job where he felt largely unsupported and unsure of the future. When he prayed again for guidance several years later and moved again, he ended up in a similar kind of insecurity, and I don't think he understood that, either. He certainly never understood the changes in his beloved Catholic Church, and to his dying day never did approve of them. I think the crowning blow was when, six months after his retirement, my mother's cancer relapsed and, after a horrible illness during which he lost forty pounds caring for her, she died. Yet through all of that, his faith never wavered. There was a centeredness about Dad that was always there. He clearly had what the Shakers call the gift.

We need to have faith in our souls, to have faith that through them we can receive the guidance we seek. It is a question of meditation, of prayer, of asking and listening.

"And when we find ourselves in the place just right . . ." That, for many of us, seems to be just the problem. We do not find ourselves in the place just right. We feel like failures as parents, we hate our jobs, we can't manage our health or our money, we feel as if we are in the wrong marriage, and so on. Don't talk to us about a mission in life!

There is something that, almost like a magic wand, can turn our wrong moments into right moments, into "the place just right." The key is to take the moment we have and to add to it the desire to know how it fits into the purpose of our lives. Once we begin to ask that question and to allow it to percolate in our souls, we have taken the "wrong" place we believe ourselves to be in and have turned it into the "place just right," a place of knowing, a place in which to encounter not the limits, but the infinite, the wisdom of God. When Job had his suffering and sorrow, the Bible tells us, he turned to God in heated anger and proclaimed his innocence and the injustice of his pain. God listened, and then he spoke. He took Job out of the narrowness of his limited thinking and gave Job the perspective that he was being cared for by the one who had created the universe and all that was in it. That opened Job's vision and changed his life.

And so it is with us. Anytime we open a wrong or limited moment to the scrutiny of our soul, the vessel of God, we are turning the place just wrong into the place just right. Any moment, if we so choose, can be a moment for encountering the divine. By turning, turning to the perspective of the one who made us, we can find ourselves in the place just right, and "by turning, turning, we come round right." That simple gift is the best gift of all. It is all we could ever want.

Chapter Fifteen

Love Is
the Miracle

⌇

*T*hat I'm not walking around like a zombie about the plumbing problems in my house is a miracle," a friend remarked to me one day. When she said that, I reflected on how much people are taken with the concept of miracles these days. How different, I thought, from the days of my youth, when miracles meant something that did not happen in people's everyday lives, but only to special people at special times.

In those days, you would ask for a miracle only

under very special circumstances, and if you did ask, you always had it in the back of your mind that the answer could be no. People would travel for miles to famous shrines, such as Fatima, Lourdes, Guadalupe, to present themselves to God for a cure, for a reconciliation, for a new job. Miracles in those days seemed like random occurrences, and although they happened in many cases, they certainly did not happen in most cases.

Miracles back then were awesome, impressive. They were defined as actions of God that involved the suspension of the natural order of things, and that could not be explained by merely natural means. A crippled person being helped into the waters at Lourdes and who emerged totally healed and able to walk would be examined by teams of physicians, who would verify that the cure was not a gimmick or capable of being explained by some natural process. That made miracles seem all the more remote to most of us. As a child, I remember visiting the Shrine of the North American Martyrs in Midland, Ontario, and in the chapel seeing row after row of crutches that had been abandoned by people who had been cured of various crippling maladies. Without knowing the stories of these various lives and healings, I knew instinctively that something extraordinary had taken place. I knew that I could always ask for a miracle, if need be, but I also knew that miracles were not all that frequent. In fact, they were downright mysterious. People referred to biblical times as the age of miracles, implying the rarity of such miracles today. And no one could really ever say for sure why miracles happened in some cases and not in others.

That is why my friend's remark and the current hunger for miracles in our society are all the more striking. To listen to ordinary speech today, and to read the vast amount of literature available on spirituality today, is to realize that people are truly looking for God's presence in their lives, and they expect to see it. Often when they speak of this, they use the word *miracle*.

I think it is important for us to understand that the ordinary use of the word *miracle* today lacks the precision of "miracle" as I have been describing it traditionally and officially. There are advantages and disadvantages to the less precise use of the word, but for now I would like to probe exactly what it is we are intending to say about God and ourselves as we look for what we call miracles.

People today are interested in miracles. There has been a gradual deepening of our common spiritual experience. In a very short time, we have gone from the realization that materialism does not work as a final solution to human life, to a rediscovery of the importance of mental attitude, to a rediscovery of the depths of the human soul.

The personalization of spirituality (people finding a sense of the spiritual outside of traditional religions as well as inside them) has led to a desire that miracles be available not to an elite few, but to everyone. In addition, the word *miracle* has come into vogue in everyday language. It used to be that the word *miracle* had a connotation of rarity and remoteness (they always happened to somebody else). Now they can happen to us, we feel—and we want them to.

How can you measure the importance of a miracle? It is a little like my father's definition of minor surgery: "Minor surgery," Dad used to tell me, "is surgery that is being had by someone else." On a given day, the occurrence of the smallest good thing can seem like a major miracle. I remember one extremely trying day, when all I could do was sort of doggedly pray and put it all in the hands of God. When I got home, there was a package waiting from a listener, someone I had never met and who had met me only on the radio. The package contained a note written by hand on some yellow lined paper. The note explained that she had heard *As You Think* and wanted to make a donation but could not afford to. Instead, she was giving me some hand-sewn pictures she had purchased, which she hoped would brighten my life. One of the pictures I will never forget. It portrayed a little girl carrying an umbrella. Stitched above the umbrella were the words BE NICE TO ME. I HAVE HAD A HARD DAY. Those pictures, some of them in frames that were falling apart, meant so much to me that day. In addition to being an expression of her kindness, they were an expression of God's love and concern, and his promise that tomorrow would be a better day. A miracle? Maybe not, but it sure seemed like one.

Do miracles happen only by chance, or are they something we can control? Is it true that some people are "just lucky" or perhaps "divinely favored" and have all sorts of miracles in their lives, while we sit by the sidelines and experience nothing at best and bad luck at worst?

We are funny creatures. We claim that we want to be well, that we want to be successful, that we want to have a happy and fulfilled life, but how often we sabotage ourselves and keep ourselves from doing it. Then we sit and complain that nothing good ever happens to us, that no one ever gives us a break, that we are alone and have no one to care for us. Then we begin to complain that others get all the breaks and get the things we want.

When do miracles actually happen? Ordinarily, we think of miracles as taking place when we actually get what we want. I remember one week when I did not have the money for the week's radio program. Just before we went on the air, my producer,

Ric Sansone, handed me an envelope. In it was a check from a new sponsor, more than enough for the week. When did the miracle happen? The answer seems obvious: It happened when I received the envelope, right?

Wrong, I think. From the viewpoint of soul, the miracle happened when I finally began to trust that God would guide me toward meeting all of my needs. *That* was the miracle, not the check. The miracle always takes place within; after that, anything wonderful can happen.

It is tempting for us to take a shallow, superficial view of miracles, and to see them in terms of the external favors we are granted. Doing that to God is a little like marrying someone for their money. We often treat miracles in much the same way, and in so doing shortchange both God and our souls. We follow God not for the depth of the relationship, but for the things he can do for us on the outside.

Miracles happen not when external results take place, but when an internal change takes place in the depths of the soul. Miracles happen when the soul learns to put its trust in God and enters into the beauty and the immeasurable depth of a relationship with him.

Failing to understand that, we often chafe at the spiritual bit when our prayers seem not to be answered. We rant and rave, wondering why God is not answering our prayers. After all, we have done no wrong. It must be God's fault.

"The fault, dear Brutus, lies not with the stars, but with ourselves." Often enough, when we find we are not getting results, we may be looking for the wrong results. We may also be looking for the results in the wrong place.

In a society that relies so much upon productivity, numbers, and results, we often lose sight of the fact that miracles happen not when the results occur, but when the person deepens on the inside. Miracles happen in the soul. When we are asking for miracles, we should be looking first and primarily for a miracle in the soul.

What constitutes such a miracle?

Clearly, miracles have a lot to do with a change in consciousness and with a deeper awareness of life. People who have been spared their lives, having suffered a nearly fatal illness, are often deeply aware of having been given a second chance: They treasure life now in a new way. They use their time more wisely and are more focused. They have a greater sense of what is important in life and what is trivial. Clearly, they have a new level of wisdom about life.

The true essence of a miracle is not found simply in knowledge or consciousness. If it were that only, then miracles could be produced by a technique. We could follow this or that procedure, and a miracle would appear. Most of us have met with the disappointment of "doing everything just right" in asking for a miracle and finding that the miracle we asked for didn't seem to happen. Miracles are not the result of consciousness alone or of methods alone. In the final analysis, love is the miracle.

When we are looking for miracles, it is tempting to turn our thoughts straight toward the thing we want. There is nothing wrong with that; it's just that it gives us less than we can have and less than we really need. When we ask for the thing we want, and ask for love at the same time, we render ourselves receptive to the higher wisdom of the soul, the wisdom of God.

When we turn our thoughts only to what we are asking for, we may find ourselves befuddled and angry when we do not appear to get the miracle we want. The real miracle is love. St. Augustine's dictum "Love, and do what you will" often sounds like a saintly invitation to a promiscuous life. On the contrary, when we really love, our lives become very responsible. It is amazing to see ourselves deepen and change over the years as we mature in love. As we mature and develop a sense of why we're here, love guides and directs us toward a responsible life.

Can we control miracles, or are they utterly beyond our management? The answer to both questions is yes. Contrary to popular belief, praying for a miracle need not be a matter of simply throwing a request into the air and hoping God is in a good mood or back from vacation. We can realize the desires of our hearts and are in a better position to do so when we underpin them with love. In some of the prosperity literature, it is often suggested that when people make affirmations for a particular good that they desire, they append the following phrase to their prayer: "This or something better." When we fuel our petitions with love, we are willing to accept the more loving thing, even when it is different from what we thought we wanted. When Ignatius of Loyola was instructing his companions in the newly founded Jesuits, he told them that in all their decisions, they should choose the things that were more for the greater glory of God, more in the direction of divine love. Add to that bit of wisdom an insight from Augustine, who compared love to a weight that draws us to the object of our desire. "My love is my weight," he said. When we have given our lives totally to love, to God (as Ignatius suggests), we are drawn to it (as Augustine suggests), wherever it may be found. When there are competing loves, we choose the one that is more in the direction of love, more to the glory of God.

When I said a moment ago that we are totally out of control in love at the same time that we are controlling the direction of our love, I was not kidding. That is the paradox of love. We choose to love, and often enough find ourselves being drawn in whole other directions. The Sufi poet Rumi remarks upon the wandering course of love: "A lover is always accused of something. But when he finds his love, whatever was lost in the looking comes back completely changed."

Those changes are sometimes dramatic and deep. At the moment, the miracle contained in them may be far from evident. At those times, life invites us to widen our vision to see the miracle that is being offered. There is always a miracle, although it may not be the miracle we were looking for.

When my mother became ill with cancer for the second time, my father nursed her and cared for her until the hour of her death. It broke his heart to see her in her weakened condition and in so much pain, and he lost forty pounds in the process. He was following the course of love.

Their last Thanksgiving, when my mother was unable to walk, unable to cook, and was ravaged by weeks of chemotherapy, she burst into tears and exclaimed, "I have lost all my dignity." Where was the miracle in that unbearable moment? my father wondered.

It was three weeks in coming, but it came. It came in the form of one of the most peaceful deaths I have seen. My presence when it happened was itself something of a miracle. My parents chose to deal with my mother's illness as they had dealt with so much else in their lives: alone together, and it was clear that even I was not to be part of it. Knowing them, I made the difficult decision to respect their wishes. When Dad finally called me in New York to come home to Missouri, I literally could not find them to return his call. Unbeknownst to me, they had checked into a motel because my mother could no longer manage the stairs in their apartment. When I called, I learned that they had even checked out of the motel and into the hospital, and I had to go on the vague impressions of the motel manager to find them. When at last I walked into my mother's hospital room, I was shocked to see her. Having attended the sick and the dying as a priest, I saw immediately that my mother was truly dying. As I approached her bed, she came out of her coma. She looked at my father and said, "Paul." She looked at me and said, "Paul." Then she said, "Now it is complete," and returned to her coma.

That afternoon, while my father attended to other matters, I had some time alone with Mom. As I had done with so many dying and comatose patients, I held her hand and talked to her, keenly aware that this was not just another dying patient—this was my mother. I was blessed with the miracle of being able to say good-bye.

Two hours later, my father and I were at her bedside praying the rosary, my parents' favorite prayer. We finished, and just then my mother opened her eyes and sat up. Her eyes were clear blue, upturned, and they had that look I had known from childhood, that look of knowing that came when she had finally figured something out. She relaxed her shoulders, fell back onto her pillow, and died.

For my mother, the miracle was that she had gone to God surrounded by the two people she loved more than anything. Her suffering was over, and she had found the God she had sought all her life.

For my father, the miracle was that his beloved Helen did not have to suffer anymore. It was not the miracle he had wanted, the miracle of having her well, of enjoying his hard-earned retirement with her.

For me, it was the miracle of being there, of not being excluded from my mother's pain, but finally having a part in her last agony. It was the miracle of saying good-bye—and especially the miracle of saying thank you for her seventy-four years of dedication and love. Four years later, when I myself was near death, I discovered another miracle. In her peaceful dying, Mom had taught me not to be afraid of death; and when it looked as if my time, too, had come, I discovered that I was not fearful.

All three of us had prayed for the miracle of Mom's recovery. That miracle was not granted to us. Instead, we received the miracle of being together as a family—beyond time and space, beyond flesh and bloodlines, beyond life and death—forever. The other miracles I have mentioned clustered around one another to give birth to that final miracle, which will never pass away.

We understand the ways of love when and only when we have found a home in love, and, paradoxically, when love has found a home in us. Prosperity literature often advises that we should claim our good in our hearts before we actually possess it. The deeper wisdom behind this is that when we are living in love, what we are seeking actually seeks us. We are attracted to it, and it is attracted to us. We transform it, and it transforms us. That is because love unifies; that is its whole purpose. Hence Elizabeth Barrett Browning declared, "I love thee with the depth and breadth and height my soul can reach/When, feeling out of sight,/For the ends of Being and ideal grace."

So what are we to make of miracles? It seems to me we need both kinds of miracles: the rare, official miracles and the everyday, readily available miracles. We need the official ones because they remind us of the majesty and specialness of God's love in our lives. They take miracles out of the realm of the ordinary and, in an age that tends to see miracles as ordinary, remind us that God's interventions are very special.

But I am grateful for the everyday miracles as well. I am glad that we can more than hope for God's intervention in our lives, that we can actually come to rely on it. Miracles make me realize that the unpredictability of life can actually be a favorable thing. They can help me remember that God's trickery can be delightful and endearing and life giving. And, finally, everyday miracles wake me up to the fact that there is more to life than meets the eye. They encourage me not to settle for the least common denominator in life. They challenge and invite me to give my entire life over to love, to the divine. And they teach me that when I do that, I have a permanent and enchanting home, both in my soul and in the world outside my soul. It is the very world for which I was created, the world of love.

Would you like to have a miracle? Love is the miracle.

Chapter Sixteen

You Are Attractive

~~~

have always been fascinated with magnets and anything magnetic. When I was a kid, I remember sending some cereal boxtops to an appointed address and receiving back a compass ring, which, to my mother's great amusement, I referred to as a "com*pass* ring." When the magical ring appeared, I slipped it onto my finger and marveled at how the tip of the arrow always pointed north. In the presence of magnets, I would be entertained for hours, watching iron filings, metallic buttons, paper clips, blades of scissors, all sorts of ordinary objects, come alive in the presence of a magnet. Later, of course, I learned about the law of gravity, and discovered that the universe was a magnet, and that our weight was caused by that magnetic force.

Later, as I became interested in language, I began to notice turns of phrase that alluded to magnets and gravity. I heard about "the gravity of the situation." I met people who had "magnetic personalities." Certain individuals were described as being "physically attractive" or "repulsive."

Gravity is a natural, physical process, and by and large in our society we do not pay sufficient attention to that fact. We seem to think that gravity is natural when it comes to physical objects, but a matter of chance when it comes to persons. How many times have we heard someone described as "lucky" when he or she is physically attractive or has a magnanimous personality. "Some people get all the breaks," we say, and we lament that such charming, outgoing physiques and spirits somehow managed not to fall our way.

The truth is, magnetism is a natural process, whether physical or spiritual, whether predicated on things or persons. Quantum physics tells us that everything is made up of energy and information that forms into the so-called "solid" realities we experience. This means that there is an attractive force holding the bits of energy and information in everything that we see and hear, touch and taste and smell. Classical metaphysics tells us that, whatever definition of being you prefer, everything that exists participates in the nature of being and for that reason has some sort of inner cohesiveness. Idealists, who believe that reality exists only as ideas in our minds, have to account for why ideas combine with one another or repel one another.

Attraction, then, is something natural. Even given the fact that some objects repel other objects, one could think of that repulsion as a force that gets an object as far away from Point A as possible and that thereby drives it into an attractiveness to something else somewhere else.

It often does not occur to us that attraction is a normal and natural part of life. We are not used to thinking of things as clusters of relationships. We are most certainly not used to thinking of ourselves as clusters of relationships. We tend to regard our relationships as though they were completely outside of ourselves, having little or no connection with our inner life. If our relationships go well, we think of ourselves as lucky. Or if they do not go well, we might both let it reflect upon our personal lack of luck and blame our misfortune on others.

Part of being human is to attract others. We

cannot help attracting others to ourselves. We are, by nature, social beings; we mingle and interact constantly and of necessity with others. Moreover, we need to realize that our attractions are not a matter of chance, nor a matter of the caprice or choice of others. Gravity and magnetism are natural, and when someone or something is in our life, it is there for a reason.

We do not realize this sufficiently because we do not understand the power that lies deep within us: the power of our thoughts. People often think that the reality outside of themselves determines their thoughts, and to a certain extent it does. But far more important is the power of our thoughts to shape and determine our external reality. What the Bible says is true: "As you think, so shall you be." Our prejudices, our expectations, our beliefs, shape ourselves and our world. And magnetism is the reason for it.

Just as iron filings cluster around a magnet, so our external world clusters around our attitudes and beliefs about ourselves and our world. When people believed that it was impossible to sail around the world, they amassed many reasons to defend their position. It took a Columbus to challenge the fundamental idea of the impossibility, to gather a different set of ideas around that hypothesis and then to act on that cluster.

I love to interview Les Brown, the motivational

speaker, author, and talk-show host. Every time I am with him, my spirits soar. His story is a testimonial to the magnetic power of faith.

Growing up in an extremely poor neighborhood in Detroit, Les Brown seemed destined for a life going nowhere. Not only did he have the normal disadvantages of urban poverty, he was diagnosed as educably mentally retarded. The stigma of that diagnosis burned in his soul, to the point where he used it routinely to explain his inabilities. One day, as Les stammered his way through a presentation in front of his schoolmates, the teacher refused to accept the excuse and insisted that the young man continue his recitation.

"But I can't," the discouraged boy replied. "I'm educably mentally retarded."

"Don't you ever say that again," the teacher barked. And he insisted that Les go on.

The presentation was far from sterling, but the teacher had faith in his young pupil and worked with him with unwavering conviction. Many years later, that teacher turned on his television and saw there, as an adult, the motivational speaker Les Brown standing on a stage motivating others. Open a window in a person's soul and let in the fresh air of a new idea, and that person's influence upon the world can multiply a hundredfold.

Of course, the idea must be supported by conviction and hard work. But what is important here is the power of an idea. One good idea can literally change reality. Allow ideas of impossibility to be replaced by ideas of opportunity coupled with ideas of interest and dedication, and suddenly the right doors fly open, the right people appear, and reality begins to arrange itself around the new idea. Allow an idea to be coupled with ideas of self-doubt, of impossibility, of fear, of lack of resources, or of hidebound dedication to what "everyone knows" can be done, and negativism literally chokes the innovation to death.

Ideas have power. They are magnetic. Every idea draws that unto itself that will help it to accomplish what it stands for, and tends to reject those that oppose it.

Ideas are magnetic even to the souls they reach. Ideas tend to draw to themselves the souls that will give them a home, and to repel those that will not. We see this every day when we are tempted. If I am really hungry and am tempted to steal a loaf of bread, my mind and my heart will amass all sorts of ideas supportive of stealing that loaf. If I give in, the force of habit will make it easier for me to give in the next time, and the next. Pretty soon, I have become a thief, and ideas of stealing have found a home in me.

I learned this very personally one summer when I was doing some typing for my dad in his office. His secretary was on vacation, and he needed typing done, so I went in to do it. Someone came into the office and remarked to my dad how surprised he was that I could type. I remember overhearing my dad say, "Well, he is so awkward with his hands, we wanted to give him something he could do easily with his hands." My dad didn't even know I had heard the remark, and while I wouldn't say that it scarred me for life, it was nonetheless deeply hurtful. I was pretty confused and diffident, and the remark flew like a homing pigeon into my turbulent soul. It quite reinforced in me the notion of my personal clumsiness and comes back to me every now and then when I think about buying something I have to assemble, or am doing something more complicated than changing a lightbulb.

I thought about the power of old and new ideas one summer when I was helping with a regional conference of the North American Conference of Separated and Divorced Catholics. There were some 200 people who attended that conference. Some of them had been separated or divorced less than a year; others had been divorced for two decades or more. Having that mix of people was very helpful for everyone. The recently divorced people drew on the wisdom of those ahead of them, and came to understand that their lives were by no means over simply because they were divorced. Those who had been divorced a long time learned how to mentor the others, learned how much they had to give to others. Those in between began to realize that they were no longer beginners, and that they had grown greatly in the time since the trauma of divorce first entered their lives. Over the weekend, I noticed that people gravitated to those whom they could learn from, and to those whom they could help. There was a magnetism that gave everyone the contacts and the ideas they needed in order to grow.

If ideas are magnetic, then we who have them are magnetic as well. We are a special kind of magnet, for we get to choose the directions and contents of our magnetism. I can choose to pay attention to the cluster of ideas that would lead me to steal the bread. Or I can choose to pay attention to ideas that will lead me to earn the money to buy the bread. It's up to me.

It seems that we do not choose all of the ideas and clusters that come our way. Les Brown, for example, did not choose the ideas that told him he was mentally retarded. He did choose to act upon them, to act as if they were not true, but that was only because, as a child, he did not have other information. We act upon the information that is at our disposal. Once his mother and his teacher gave him new information, he had to decide to trust the new ideas and to pay attention to them.

Similarly, we have to discern what information

we are going to pay attention to and which we are not. It is a source of maturity when we begin to evaluate for ourselves the stories we are receiving about life, about our world, about ourselves. Are we buying into reality, or are we being sold the Brooklyn Bridge? In this information age, we get all sorts of falsehoods, rumors, likelihoods, and possibilities all mixed in with honest-to-goodness truths. That is why we need to have within ourselves a "truth detector," something that enables us to draw the truth toward ourselves and to repel the falsehoods.

We do have such a truth detector. I learned this as a small kid when I once tried lying to my mother. I forget at the moment what jam I had gotten myself into, but whatever it was, I certainly did not want her to find out. So I made up a very convincing story that completely exonerated me from any blame. Any fool could see how completely innocent I was. Not my mother. She saw right through the story and through me, and I was punished both for what I had done and for telling a lie. That taught me a great lesson: Mothers have a truth detector that is not to be defied.

What is that truth detector that we have inside us? We call it by many names, depending on how we are gong to use it, but it is always a function of soul. We call it our critical faculty or taste when we are reading literature or attending a concert or a play that we either like or do not like. I am always amused whenever I hear the classical saying that "there is no disputing about tastes." As a matter of fact, we dispute about little else. Go to a wine-tasting sometime, and bring a friend. You think the muscatel is wonderful; she hates it but loves the Chablis, and so the evening goes. Go to a movie. You think it is wonderful; she thinks it has too many special effects. Taste governs a great deal of our lives, and it is decidedly one of the things that we do argue about.

But our choices and decisions, what we draw to ourselves and what we repel, are not matters of taste alone. When it comes to our moral choices, our decisions must not be based merely on our preferences, no matter how well informed they might be. When it comes to moral decisions, we look to something called conscience, which is another aspect of soul. The word *conscience* literally means "knowing with," and it refers to the human ability to weigh moral alternatives and to make moral decisions. Conscience is an extremely important aspect of soul, because it determines the moral environment in which human beings make their daily choices—whether to behave in ways that are right or wrong.

What is conscience anyway? Most of us think of it as a kind of Jiminy Cricket or internal computer that gives us instant moral guidance. I prefer to think of conscience as an atmosphere in which moral decisions are made. To me, the atmosphere of conscience is the soul itself: The soul is the home of conscience. The best way to make good moral decisions is to develop the soul and to live soulfully. As I say this, I think of all the people who advised me to take a broad liberal arts curriculum when I was a student in college. We were just beginning the era when everybody wanted to go into science or business and thought that liberal arts were just a waste of time. I did take the liberal arts program, and have been grateful ever since. It gave me a love of the arts that awakened my soul and touched the rest of my life. Perhaps that is why I am so insistent that developing the soul is the best foundation for moral decision making. We tend to make important life decisions much too quickly these days. In some cases, it is because we apply rules too quickly without reference to the complexity of the situation. In other cases, it is because people believe that there are no moral standards and that these decisions should be left entirely up to the individual to make. To me, both approaches are devoid of soul.

Conscience needs a home, and the soul is its home. One of the problems with moral decision making in our society is that often enough, conscience is wandering around homeless, looking for a place to anchor. We are constantly telling one another, "Follow your conscience," but it is very hard to follow something that is rootless. The Bible often talks about people who are like "sheep without a shepherd," and while we are not a rural society anymore, we instantly understand what that means. We understand Shakespeare, too, when he says, "Conscience doth make cowards of us all." Suffering, we are looking for a place to lick our wounds and to be comforted. Intelligent in an information-oriented society, we have so much scientific and moral awareness at our fingertips, yet we realize how powerless that knowledge can make us feel. We need a home for our conscience, and that home is the soul. When you find your soul, you find the ground, the anchor, the place of solace that your conscience needs in those poignant moments when life demands a decision.

Do you also find concrete guidance? I believe you do: That, too, is part of coming home to your soul. At times when my adult life becomes confusing and painful, I would love to be able to call or even fly home to Missouri for a weekend with Mom and Dad. I can still taste my dad's banana daiquiris and his steaks on the grill on Saturdays and Mom's roast, mashed potatoes, and gravy on Sundays. I can still cherish their wisdom and smile at their funny ideas. How comforting it would be to flop again onto their couch and spend the weekend!

Mom and Dad are long gone now, and going home is no longer an option. But I still have a home to go to, and that home is my soul. In my soul there is memory, and in my mind's eye, I can travel back home on the weekends and find comfort and wisdom there. My soul is full of prayers for every occasion, and memories of prayer. My soul is full of stories and poems, some of which I have read and heard, and others of which are woven from the events of my life and on the loom of imagination. There are ideas in my soul, and I love to go within and ponder them, mix them up, combine them. There are feelings: anger, hurt, fear, depression sometimes, yes, but also love and warmth, humor and deep joy and laughter. And beneath and above and around them all, there is God: guiding, centering, balancing, unbalancing, cringing at my stupidity, rejoicing when I do something right.

In addition, there is moral guidance in my soul. I would not want to be hard and fast about this, but I think it is of two kinds. There is a moral sense, and there is also moral teaching.

First, there is a moral sense, formed out of the background of the other facets of the home that is my soul. All of my life experience works together to form the background and atmosphere in which I make my decisions. Did I grow up in a rigid or in a permissive atmosphere? Have I overcome the painful aspects of my background or am I still traumatized by them? Am I intellectually open or am I reluctant to let new ideas in? These and a thousand other things form the background, the soul, in which I make my moral decisions.

As much as we like to pretend that our ideologies are purely intellectual matters untainted by feelings, memories, and tastes, it usually doesn't happen that way. We grow in freedom insofar as we are able to recognize our leanings, our prejudices, our predominant moods, and how they affect our gathering of information and the formation of our notions. As a kid, I read a lot more stories and books on sports and much less poetry and literature than I do now. Now I could spend hours staring at a cluster of trees around a beautiful lake, but as a kid, that would have made me very restless. Then, I could hear a baseball statistic and remember it perfectly; now I tend to learn more by absorption. In school, I learned by memorizing, but in graduate school, I realized that I was learning more by the impression and feel of an idea than by its content. When someone asks me a question, the first thing that happens is that I feel the flow of concepts and then I know the answer intellectually. All of those factors influence the kinds of things I pay attention to and the kinds of answers I come up with. My approach is not the same as that of many other people. It comes out of the individuality of my soul, and so do theirs.

That moral tone is an important aspect of what we call conscience. Remember, the word comes from two Latin words meaning "to know" and "with": It means "to know with." The aspect of my knowing I have just described is the "with." I know with all of that "buzzing booming confusion" of feelings, impressions, and ideas that together form the tenor of my soul. But there is also *science*, "knowledge." When I cook, for example, I tend to cook by impression and taste, but I usually like to have a recipe handy to make sure I am doing things correctly. On occasion, just before serving a meal, I have joked about having taken a turkey out of the oven when hours before I had put a roast beef in. Fortunately, it doesn't work that way. You want things to be what they are supposed to be: That's why I keep the recipe on hand.

It's the same with moral decisions. There is a moral sense—a *con*science—but it must have something to guide and direct it. That is where moral norms come in. Depending upon their background and their religious commitment, people will take their moral norms from various places. Personally, as a Roman Catholic, mine come from the natural law, Scripture, and the teachings of the Roman Catholic Church. For others, moral norms come from other sources.

Whatever the spiritual home in which you find your soul, moral sense alone is not enough. A home in which there are no walls or boundaries is a very difficult place to live. We need to be able to tell the indoors from the outdoors, and to know the difference between the kitchen, the bathroom, and the living room. To me, that is what moral rules and regulations do for us. They give us a sense of the boundaries, and this is immensely useful in living a soulful life.

In moral decision making, as in every area of life, there is no substitute for living from the depths of one's soul. Like magnets, we attract people and ideas to ourselves. Unlike magnets, we can choose which ideas to attract and which to repel. When we make those attractions and repulsions from the depths of our soul, we derive the guidance we need to make our decisions—including the important moral decisions of our lives—well.

There is one other thing to be learned from the soul's magnetism. The idea is this: *You* are attractive.

You are attractive. Many, reading this, may choose to dismiss it at first. You and I have looked through the current magazines, seen the models, and concluded that there is nothing attractive about us. Society gives us a message loud and clear: *They* are attractive; we are, well, not. At cocktail parties or large gatherings, attractive people are the center of attention. They are elegantly dressed, suave and urbane, witty and smiling, and exude tremendous charisma and confidence. I once saw a cartoon depicting a huge man entering a cocktail party jam-packed with ordinary-sized people. A look of absolute terror is on his face, and he stands panic-stricken at the threshold of the room saying, "Yipes, grown-ups!" Most of us know the feeling, for we have had it ourselves as we have entered a conference room or a ballroom or any large gathering. We don't feel attractive at all.

Through soulful living, we can choose what and whom we attract into our lives. We are attractive in the deepest and most natural sense of the word: The nature of our soul is such that it attracts people and situations to us. We do not have to be victims of these attractions; we can choose what and whom we attract. When we learn to live soulfully, we learn to attract the people, places, and situations that are best for us, that are most in line with our mission here on earth.

You are attractive—and you can choose what you attract. Being attractive is not the same as being beautiful, but at this point it is natural to ask whether one could attract beauty to oneself and one's life. The answer is yes. First, we have to remember that we are not talking here about society's standards of beauty, which are generally very superficial. But if you take time to retreat into the depths of your soul, you will have a chance to reflect on the kind of beauty you want. If we truly live attuned to our souls, we find ourselves surrounded by a kind of graciousness and loveliness (even in the midst of sorrow and sadness, by the way) that gives us a sense of how we can live our lives on the outside, and we begin to take that sense of graciousness with us wherever we go. Not only will we be attractive—it is part of our very nature—but we will be attracting attractiveness to ourselves and to our world.

Chapter Seventeen

The Miracle of Forgiveness

*O*ne of the most common subjects I am asked about on talk radio is forgiveness. It is at the forefront of people's minds. People are concerned about forgiveness at all levels: forgiveness by God, forgiveness by other people, forgiveness of themselves, even forgiveness *of* God. A lot of this seems to come from people having been hurt, as we all have, by others. Some of it comes from the sense of having been cheated in life, not so much cheated financially or in business—though there is some of that as well.

There is no doubt about it, forgiveness is a struggle. We all have personal stories of unresolved conflict. I am not claiming any special victory over my grudges, or that I have some magic formula for forgiveness in my own life. Sometimes the hurts that others inflict on us seem undeserved and baffling. I remember my mother telling me once about an aunt of hers who simply stopped speaking to the family. Of course, since she wasn't speaking to them, she couldn't tell them why. At the moment, I am baffled by the silent hostility of a friend of ten years who as far as I know has no reason to be angry about anything. I find that hard to forgive. So when I speak about forgiveness, it is not from a pedestal high atop the rest of the human race. Forgiveness plagues me as much as it does the next person.

There is, of course, quick-fix forgiveness. We do that all the time. An errant husband sneaks home late with flowers or a box of chocolates under his arm. He smiles at his hurt or angry wife, and expects all to be forgiven. He is genuinely puzzled when the ploy doesn't work.

Sometimes, of course, it does work, at least for the time being. But it doesn't work forever. It may work once or even repeatedly, but hostilities do not stay buried, and eventually there comes a painful explosion. Often, this is all the more stunning because it seems to come over something relatively trivial. When emotional issues hang on unresolved for a long time, some small thing usually becomes "the last straw," and anger gives way to out-and-out rage.

Part of the problem in forgiving others and ourselves is that most of us need to be right. Our society places a high value on being right, and sometimes, for personal reasons, we place an excessively high value on it ourselves. The need to be right can be a tremendous obstacle, both to forgiveness of ourselves and to forgiveness of others. In adult relationships, sometimes the need to be right stems from all those childhood times when we felt embarrassed, put down, dismissed, and wrong. If a child begins to feel he has no voice and that everything he does is wrong, he will either submit passively, with anger simmering below the surface, or he will openly rebel. In either case, until he has come to terms with those feelings, he may develop a fear of being wrong and an overpowering need to be right. Being right can give one a tremendous feeling of security, and the excessive need to be right often masks a tremendous sense of insecurity.

Sometimes the need to be right may come not so much from always being told one was wrong as from the fact of a very unstable upbringing. Someone I know, whose need to be right has caused havoc in relationships, marriage, and career, came from a background of having been shifted off to schools and, in effect, abandoned. I genuinely think that person had to be right in order to cope with all that instability and rejection. What was a necessary coping skill in childhood is now highly inappropriate for an adult and is genuinely destructive.

Soulful forgiveness means giving up the need to be right—or wrong—all the time. The Sufi poet Rumi once wrote: "Out beyond ideas of right-doing and wrong-doing, there is a field. I'll meet you there." In the midst of our pain over present and past hurts, can we allow ourselves to journey to the field that lies beyond judgments of right and wrong?

One day, when I was in my office, the telephone rang and a voice I did not know said, "Father Paul Keenan? I'm Stuart Walker." Stuart had received my name through a mutual business associate, and called me to share with me the news of a foundation he had established, Servants of Love. As we talked about his work of evangelization, he told me the story of his daughter Laura and her tragic death in an automobile accident just months before. She was eighteen years old, and as Stuart spoke of her, it was clear to me that she was a truly beautiful young woman, full of life and full of the love of Christ. He offered to send me a picture of her, a picture I am looking at now as I write. It is the picture of a stunningly beautiful young woman in the prime of her life. Her smile goes right through your heart.

As Stuart and I spoke, it turned out to be much more than a business call. How, I wondered, could he ever have coped with the loss of such a beautiful young daughter whom he obviously loved so much? Clearly it had not been easy. But, propelled by Laura's love and the love of God, Stuart organized his foundation, Servants of Love, to spread the Christian message to everyone he met. He prepared a video presentation, *Her Name Was Laura*, to memorialize her and to invite others to share her spirit in their own lives. And he prepared a beautiful card with Laura's picture, her writing about children, and a beautiful song that her friend Matt Moran had written and sung at her funeral, "Laura's Eyes."

When I got off the phone with Stuart, I wondered, Could I have done that? Could I have survived the loss of a child to whom I had given life and who had given life to so many? Would I be able to forgive life, to forgive God? Would I be able to go on?

Stuart was not in denial; he had had his moments of darkness, grieving, and loss. Yet he made a choice not to stay in darkness. He established a foundation to help others, and he put his heart and soul into running it.

Stuart's story shows the relationship between forgiveness and freedom. In this case, Stuart had to forgive life in order to be able to go on. He had to make a decision not to spend the rest of his life in gloom and misery; he had to journey to the field beyond right-doing and wrong-doing and come to peace there. It is clear that he is still grieving, and that he will grieve for some time. I doubt that the pain of Laura's death will ever fully go away. But Stuart made a conscious choice to go on, and to use the tragedy of Laura's death as a way to help others.

Soulfulness for Stuart was making a free decision to go on. It touched Stuart's life in another way as well. Stuart's free decision to found Servants of Love enabled him to live relatively unhindered by the past and by bad feelings. So often today we hear of people who are scarred by their past and do not seem to be able to get beyond it. We are so accustomed to these stories that it has become commonplace to hear people blame their present lot on their personal past. There is no question that a dysfunctional childhood can tend to make one repeat the behavior one experienced. Our scars from childhood and from adult traumas can affect us deeply for the rest of our lives. What we do not hear so often—and what comes out so clearly in Stuart's story—is that we can make a decision to free ourselves from the pain of the past, even from our own mistakes in the past. Like Stuart, we can go on and live a life full of love.

It is not an easy decision to come to. Approaching forgiveness too soon can really convey the message that we want to shut down or shut off the other person's feelings, which are real and legitimate to them. Particularly if someone has been given the message that they are no good or always wrong or incompetent, too quick an effort to establish forgiveness can simply cause yet one more failure and its concomitant feelings. "I'm a failure at relationships. I'm a failure at forgiveness. And to be a failure at forgiveness makes me a bad person." Those may not be the realities, but they are the feelings one often has.

The decision to forgive, the decision to be free, is ours alone. It does not require the assistance or initiative of anyone else, other than God. That is why I say that we need to think more in our society about the difference between forgiveness and reconciliation. When we insist that the other person apologize first before we forgive, it is not the other person we hold in bondage; it is ourselves. Even if other people do nothing at all to extend a reconciling hand or even to admit that they were wrong, we can detach ourselves from the hurt and pain. We can release other people to the path they are on, ask God to help them, and move along.

What is involved in this kind of freedom? How can we develop it for ourselves? How can we be free from the pain of what others have done to us recently or in the past? How can we be free from the results of the regrets we have over things we have done to others? How can we forgive others even when they do nothing to extend themselves to us or to admit a part in what happened?

The first step, I believe, is release. We need to release ourselves, our pain, our hurt, along with the other person, into the hands of God. "I would rather die than release that person into the hands of God," you say. What you need to realize is that if you do not release them, you will indeed die, perhaps not physically, but at least spiritually. Increasingly, doctors are realizing how many of our chronic headaches, back pains, and other ongoing complaints are due to the emotional baggage we are carrying around with us. And it is not only complaints: There is a growing belief that some life-threatening diseases, such as cancer and heart attack, are due to severe emotional distress. There is growing evidence that when we hold tight to our negative and hurtful feelings, we are physically and spiritually dying.

When we hold a grudge or hang on to painful memories, we sometimes speak as though we were avenging the person who has harmed us. The plain truth is, we are only harming ourselves. The Lord's Prayer, which asks, "Forgive us our trespasses as we forgive those who trespass against us," is perfect psychology as well as perfect spirituality. We will be released from much of our physical and emotional pain only after we have released those who have harmed us into the hands of God. When we do not, we are only hurting ourselves.

Soulful forgiveness means release. It also means allowing ourselves the freedom to use our experiences to live well and to make the world a better place. No matter whether the other person makes a move first, we can, without denying our feelings of anger and hurt, assure ourselves that these feelings need not cripple us, but actually aid us in our God-given mission of transforming ourselves— and our world.

Chapter Eighteen

Finding
Your Soul

What are we saying when we say the word *I*? It is very confusing. On the one hand, we are talking about all of the identities, all of the names and feelings and people and attractions and repulsions, that form our lives. Me, I like music, I get up at six every morning, I love to cook. Among artists of note, I love Monet and El Greco the most. Schoenberg's "Transfigured Night" is my favorite composition. I love the computer, hate the telephone, can sit for hours staring at a tree or a skyline. City noises are my background. Quiet is my favorite time of day.

Who am I, anyway? Am I the rush home to feed my cats, the breathless subway ride to the next talk or talk show or taping or dinner? Am I the overcrowded appointment book, the grouchy wait for the elevator, the tranquillity of my pipe, the weary dive into my bed at night? Am I the warm, cherishing presence of my friends? The jangling annoyance of a pest?

Am I the sum total of all that? Or am I none of that, really?

From time to time, I take a lot of heat about the Catholic Church's teaching on evolution. The pope said a while back that Catholics could believe in evolution, and a few weeks later, Cardinal O'Connor said from the pulpit that Adam and Eve might have been lower creatures into which God infused a human soul. Being a priest and a talk-show host, I took a lot of angry phone calls on the subject of evolution. People wondered how the pope or Cardinal O'Connor could have said the things they did.

Secretly, I smiled at all the Sturm und Drang. Smiled, because I wondered whether a lot of the anger about the suggestion that we could have evolved from lower forms of life might not be masking a hidden fear about our human condition. For it seems to me that a considerable number of us are living lives that are subhuman, and we are aching to find our way to the greatness to which we are called as human beings. When we complain about how people treat us, when we complain about our schedules, when we complain about the hand life has dealt us, we are really complaining that we do not feel very human.

That is not a fact that we acknowledge happily. We talk a great deal about quality of life, but many of us do not feel that we are living up to our potential. We talk about being made in the image and likeness of God, but we feel that we are being treated like dirt.

Martin Buber told us years ago that there was a great difference between feeling like a thing and feeling like a person. He warned us that we were losing the sense of mystery in our everyday encounters with one another. He reminded us not to slip into the habit of treating one another as objects rather than as mysteries. Buber described our growing tendency to treat one another as things, as an "I-It" relationship. How I hate it when I stand in a line at the grocery store or the drugstore, and the clerk doesn't even bother to say "Thank you" or even treats me in a surly way. When I get this treatment from my doctor or my clergyperson, I am even more irate. It is so easy for us to fall into this habit in our rushed and automated society, but we hate it when it happens to us.

The kind of treatment we like, the kind that truly respects us as human persons, Buber called "I and Thou." *Thou* is a word we struggle to understand in English. We have learned to say "you" instead, and so have lost the sense of intimacy that the word implies. Saying "you" is rather symptomatic of our tendency to impersonalize: It implies that the mystery of the other person has been agglomerated into the general mass of humanity.

Saying "thou" implies the recognition of a soul. It means that we recognize that there is an invisible, yet real and somehow palpable, uniqueness in the other person. Indeed, we do not find our soul until we have learned to find the souls of others. How easy it is to stay above the human fray, to steep ourselves in gossip, in judgment, in condemnation. How "cool" and "together," it seems, to stay to ourselves and be "above all that." Yet the truth is, you do not begin to live—you can never find your soul—until your heart has been broken by a senseless tragedy that has befallen another, until you have loved and had your love tested, until your heart has cried "Why?" because someone you love is suffering and you can't take their suffering away.

I thought I was a good teacher until the rainy Saturday afternoon on which four of my students were killed when their car spun out on a slippery road as they returned from a soccer game. I mean,

I had lectured clearly in their classes, hammed it up when appropriate, brought the eternal truths of philosophy and theology forcefully to their young minds. Yet as their crumpled bodies were pried from the wreckage, I had to realize and admit that I had never known those kids. I had taught them about the great questions of life and had completely missed their souls. Now I met their girlfriends, found out who their buddies were, listened to their sobbing parents. Now, I realized, I was finding out what I should have been finding out all along: that each of those young people was a person whom others profoundly cherished. My own narrowness of soul had kept me from ever seeing their souls, from ever knowing them. That day, I vowed that I would never deliberately let that happen again.

So, twenty years later, when a listener tells me that I heard him or her or another caller and treated them with compassion and love, I know it is at least in part because of four kids whose bright young souls went home to God, and, as they did, left me a legacy.

In our society, impersonalization is more available to us than soulfulness, and we become accustomed to treating one another impersonally. Instinctively, we want to do better, but we slip into the old patterns and habits. We get busy and we lose the sense of who we really are.

Unless we attune ourselves to paying attention to soul, it is easy to miss. You can't weigh or measure a soul, at least in the ordinary ways. When someone dies and the soul leaves the body, the body weighs the same as it did when alive; you don't subtract three pounds for the soul. We pass one another in the train station or in our cars on the thruway or in the foyer of our building and we never guess that whoever we see might be in despair, or bankrupt, or worried, or tense. Unless we are attuned to the presence of the soul, we can miss it. When we miss it, we miss what life is all about.

One reason that we often fail to notice the soul is that it is invisible or, better, unavailable to the five senses. We love to observe, and to count and measure what we observe. If we can't measure something, we say it doesn't "count." We are an eminently practical society, and we want to be shown. As a result, we tend to miss whole dimensions of life and of reality that are beyond what is observable, countable, or even fully nameable. We even name and categorize our inner life—its moods, its complexes, its neuroses. We have a name for everything.

As a result, we tend to deal with the question that began this chapter—What are we saying when we say the word *I*?—by listing birthplaces, jobs, surnames, responsibilities, and salaries. We pretend that they say it all. If you read the personal ads in the neighborhood penny savers, you see the contradiction by which so many of us live. On the one hand, there is a cry for intimacy, a need to be loved uniquely. And on the other, there is the insistence that such a love must be given by someone of a defined ethnic background, marital status, and set of interests. Call if you fit my categories.

Somewhere along the way, we have extinguished the sense of mystery in life, the appreciation of what cannot be defined or categorized. We have attempted to rein in the invisible. And yet, the invisible, mystery, the immeasurable, refuses to be confined or extinguished. Like a trickster, it pops out at us; it catches us unawares. Just when we think we have everything plotted and planned, the unthinkable and unpredictable leaps out at us and rearranges our hopes and dreams, reroutes our life.

The mystery of life refuses to be ignored. When we try to confine it or define it, it stridently insists that we notice it, in fact that we give it our undivided attention. Robert Burns's saw about "the best-laid schemes of mice and men" is familiar to us not only in our poetry books, but in our lives as well. We can write it off as fate or bad luck, ignore it and refuse to think about it, but the unpredictable mystery of life is there nonetheless, helping us to meet just the right people when we least expect to meet them, and putting us in embarrassing situations at the oddest times.

Most of us tend to become very angry and frustrated about this mysterious trickster quality of life. We feel like victims and pawns of an invisible force. We are precise people, given to well-laid plans or at least well-founded certainties, and we resent having to be victims of forces that we cannot see, schedule, or control.

Individually and as a people, we need to pay more attention to what we cannot see. We would discover that the mystery of life, when treated with attention and respect, can be a powerful source of guidance. It becomes like an enemy and plays bizarre tricks when it has been ignored, and needs to kick and scream to get our attention.

Never am I more poignantly aware of this than when I preside at healing services for families who have lost babies through stillbirth, miscarriage, or abortion. I never fail to be touched at these services as I stand in the front of the church or chapel and see it filled with grieving parents, sobbing, angry, lost. They are harder on themselves than I could ever be. Without the eyes of soul, they would be as hopeless as they believe themselves to be when they enter the church. But when I and the others on the team can show them that our hearts are broken for them, that their pain is ours, that where they need the understanding and mercy of

God it can be theirs, and that they can go on to live productive, happy, soulful lives, there is no other time when I feel so profound a joy. They come professing what they think is "obvious"— that they are evil or unlucky or hopeless—and they leave having learned that they can go beyond the "obvious" and begin to live again.

While I do not find myself delighted with every manifestation of the current interest in angels, I am delighted by the fact that we are interested in angels again. It means that our society is beginning to look beyond what can be seen, touched, and measured, and can see the possibility of spiritual guidance. During the '70s and '80s, there seemed to be a deemphasizing of the role of angels and saints in many of our religions. While it is true that the focus of religion must be primarily on God, it seems to me that we lose an important dimension of our lives when we deny or diminish a sense of connection with angels and saints. They are part of the network of spiritual guidance; we need their wisdom and intercession. And the presence of saints allows us the realization that we will always have a role to play in the betterment of the world, even after we die. Our mission does not end when we leave the earth; our souls will continue to influence those who will follow us in generations to come.

We become wise when we learn how very much

we need the guidance that comes from within. In other words, we need a soulful life. The presence of God in the very depths of our souls leads us to discover our mission and the avenues that are open for us to fulfill it. Our souls literally move heaven and earth to get us to pay attention to what we are here on earth to be and to do. In ways that are sometimes maddening to others, the soul directs our attention to the oddest things and away from the things that everyone else thinks we should be interested in. I didn't know it at the time, but my academic trouble in graduate school was my soul's way of telling me not to move in the direction of an academic career, but to find a different direction as a priest and broadcaster. Somehow, through the divine presence within, my soul knew exactly where it was being called to go. At the time I felt awful about the way things were turning out. It took some time before I realized that what appeared to be a disaster was really a wake-up call to listen to a deeper guidance.

It takes courage to believe that we are being guided when it seems that our life is in ruins. To look at a kid who is failing and unhappy in school and to see the image of a successful, happy adult is more than most parents and educators these days can manage. When I was doing volunteer reading for the blind, I met a young man who was struggling to make ends meet as a neophyte actor. I thought it remarkable that, given his difficult financial situation, he would be doing volunteer work. "Oh yes," he replied, "it is important for me to do this. This is my way of giving something to the universe. I know that the universe will give it back to me." It was his way of expressing his conviction that he had a sense of mission in his life and that he was able to find guidance from a higher power. He was able to see beyond the struggling actor to the actor with his name on a prominent marquee.

When we learn to expect that we are guided from within, and when we learn to pay attention to that guidance, our lives take on a whole new dimension. When we focus on the depths of our soul and the divine guidance that lies within us, we can find ourselves developing a patience when the storms of life arise. We can find ourselves pausing during a crisis to ask, "What am I supposed to learn from this?" "Where am I being led?" "How does this experience help me to serve others?"

Doing this means taking time to pay attention to another realm of life. But it is not just another realm; it is the realm for which we are made. The point of paying attention to the "invisible" or mysterious aspect of our lives is that it is not truly just "another" realm of life. It is the aspect of our lives that drives us, that gives us our identity and purpose, and that makes our lives rich and meaningful. Taking time to pay attention to the realm of soul means taking time to focus on a purpose beyond the everyday purposes and challenges we face. Soulful purpose is also more than mere "self-discovery." Granted, when you live a soulful life, you also find your purpose and yourself. But the drive for self-discovery in our society today is often shallow, and does not lead to true depth of soul. Self-discovery frequently implies a rugged and prideful individualism that values one's own purposes above those of others. Soulful attention to one's purpose implies a gracious and harmonious attention to the well-being of all, and to one's own place in the development of that common good. In essence, being soulful means paying attention to the divine. It means a loving and trusting surrender to the purposes of God, even when those purposes do not seem to align with our own. Soulfulness even means graciousness in the face of frustration; it means having the ability to be patient when things do not seem to be going our way, and to trust that God is guiding us from within.

Soulfulness also means learning to appreciate the ways of soul, and even to enjoy them. It is hard to be joyful when things are not going our way, and when there is real tragedy in our lives. But when we realize that we are guided and protected by God from within, we can come to wonder at how the tragedies often deepen us, give us compassion and wisdom, help us to discover what is truly important, lead us in new directions and down new paths.

Learning to appreciate the mystery of life means developing reverence for the sacredness of life. It means taking time to appreciate beauty. It means understanding that the ways of soul take their own course and follow their own timetable. Our egos urge us to rush, to repair, to get things done quickly. Our souls meander; they muse. They give us tasks that seem to divert us from our projects and goals, and then they ask us to trust that these apparent diversions are really on the high road after all. Our souls can madden us and infuriate us. Their ways are not our ways, and they refuse to let up until we learn that.

Yet our souls are our best friends. Divinely guided, they know far better than our limited minds exactly where we are supposed to be going and what we are supposed to be doing. Day and night, they dedicate themselves to our happiness, pushing and pulling us, nagging us, cajoling us, begging us to do the things that will make us truly happy.

Our souls demand that we care for them, and they are fussy about their care. Baubles, bangles, and beads are not for them. They don't mind them, necessarily, but what they thrive on and insist upon are less tangible things like beauty, peace, loyalty, honesty, freedom, truth, and love—the things of God.

Though they are sometimes bossy, our souls are truly servants of God and servants of us. Their whole work is to unite us with God and with his purposes; they are ambassadors of God. They know that what is best for us, body-and-soul creatures that we are, is to do the will of God, to be as clear an image of him as we can be, and to complete our mission here on earth to the best of our ability. Our souls are servants, bringing God to us and us to God.

Our souls grieve when we lose them and rejoice when we find them. The dis-ease we feel when we have gained an earthly treasure but done it in an unscrupulous way is the sound of our soul weeping. The joy we feel when we have done an unpleasant task with nobility and dignity is the joy of the soul.

As we deepen and grow in life, we learn to listen more attentively to those voices of soul. When the Psalmist cries, "Incline your ear to me, O God" or when he beseeches, "Lord, hear my voice," he is speaking for all of us who have learned to listen to the soul as it weeps, as it rejoices, as it seeks, as it begs. As we grow in life, we learn that as strident as the voice of loneliness can be at times, beneath it is the companionship of the soul. That is why the Psalmist prays to God when he feels alone and afraid, with no one to turn to. He knows that down underneath the loneliness, there is the voice of soul, the image of God, calling, seeking, attracting, protecting.

As we, too, learn to listen to the voice of our soul within us, we see life in a different way. We gradually become at home in a new world, even as we find our way through this one. As we do this, there is a greater ease and certainty in our lives, a greater sense of purpose, a sense that we are gifted and guided, the realization that in trying to live a soulful life, we are not alone.

Acknowledgments

My special thanks to Denise Marcil, my agent, who saw a book in the few scattered pages I originally showed her, and whose help and criticism and interest and friendship have helped me through my first endeavor as an author. Thanks, too, to June Cotner, who introduced me to Denise: If books had aunts, June would be the aunt of *Good News for Bad Days*. Thanks to Mel Parker of Warner Books for his warm vote of confidence and scintillating exchanges of ideas and encouragement; and to Sharon Krassney and Dan Ambrosio of Warner for their efficient and friendly help. Thanks, too, to Joe Zwilling, director of the Office of Communications of the Archdiocese of New York, and to all of my colleagues there, who cheered me on and who daily endure my puns and practical jokes. Thank you to all my friends, to Susan Zappo and Jane Hurley, dear friends for so many years, who have always been there through thick and through thin and who are the very stuff that soulful friendship is made of. I am so grateful to God for Sisters Raymond Dieckman and Rita Redmond: They taught me Latin and English and the true meaning of friendship. Thanks to Dr. Joan Caulfield Warne and her husband, Dr. Alan Warne—to Joan for years of friendship and to both of them for the gift of renewed friendship in their life together. To my friends the Foleys—to Rick and J.J., to Liz, Caroline, Emily, Tommy, and Will—who have taught me about art and the art of soulful family-making and who have allowed me a special place in their home and in their hearts. Thanks to the Carluccis—Dr. Lenny, Chris, Marisa, and Lorianna—for the gifts of healing, fun, and friendship, and to Lenny's dedicated and wonderful staff. Thanks to Bob McGrath, so helpful as a friend and as a PR man. To Peggy Eisenhardt and her students at Holy Trinity School in Poughkeepsie, New York, whose friendship and vivaciousness have lifted my soul. Thanks to Ric Sansone, friend and *As You Think* producer, who has given so much of himself to my radio work. To Noah Fleischman, friend and *As You Think* engineer, who makes radio come alive through his powerful imagination and magnificent heart. And to Mike Sivilli of ABC, whose engineering skills and depth of soul are so remarkable. To Carol and Joe Siracusano, whose friendship and support and hard work in behalf of *As You Think* mean so much. To Darrell and Jana Emerich, whose wonderful sense of romance carries over into the lives of all who know them. To my colleagues on *Religion on the Line,* Dr. Byron Shafer and Rabbi Joseph Potasnik, and to Margaret Shafer, for their wonderful friendship and sharing of faith. To Seif and Maria Ashmawy for the wisdom of Islam and the gift of their friendship. To those many friends, too numerous to mention, whose love and encouragement have made all things possible. To my wonderful guests, many of whom have become personal friends. I think especially of Jill Burk, Wayne Dyer, Thomas Moore, Louise O'Brien, Susan RoAne, and Barbara Sher. To Father Bartholomew Daly and Sharron Charlton, Eileen Fawl and Steve Diamond, and all the wonderful people of Our Lady of Peace Church. To all who listen to and support so generously my radio ministry with their donations, their prayers, their letters and calls. Thanks to all of you, and all the blessings of living a soulful life.

Bibliography

Barks, Coleman, with Joyn Moyne. *The Essential Rumi*. San Francisco: Harper San Francisco, 1995.

Bode, Richard. *First You Have to Row a Little Boat*. New York: Warner Books, 1993.

——. *Beachcombing at Miramar*. New York: Warner, 1996.

Catechism of the Catholic Church. Washington, D.C.: United States Catholic Conference, 1994.

Coleman, Paul. *Getting to the Heart of the Matter*. Holbrook, Mass.: Bob Adams, Inc., 1994.

Cotner, June. *Graces*. San Francisco: Harper San Francisco, 1994.

Covey, Stephen R., with A. Roger Merrill and Rebecca R. Merrill. *First Things First*. New York: Simon and Schuster, 1994.

Dyer, Wayne. *Real Magic*. New York: Harper Collins, 1992.

——. *Everyday Wisdom*. Carson, Cal.: Hay House, 1993.

Frankl, Viktor. *Man's Search for Meaning*. New York: Pocket Books, 1959.

Hammarskjöld, Dag. *Markings*. New York: Alfred A. Knopf, 1968.

Himmelfarb, Gertrude. *The De-Moralization of Society*. New York: Alfred A. Knopf, 1995.

Moore, Thomas. *Care of the Soul*. New York: Harper Collins, 1992.

Redfield, James. *The Celestine Prophecy*. New York: Warner, 1994.

RoAne, Susan. *The Secrets of Savvy Networking*. New York: Warner, 1994.

Sher, Barbara. *Live the Life You Love*. New York: Delacorte, 1996.

Underhill, Evelyn. *Mysticism*. New York: Meridian Books, 1960.

Walters, J. Donald. *Secrets of Life*. New York: Warner, 1994.